THE LEADERSHIP EDGE

John Vizzuso

authorHOUSE®

AuthorHouse™
1663 Liberty Drive, Suite 200
Bloomington, IN 47403
www.authorhouse.com
Phone: 1-800-839-8640

First published by AuthorHouse 4/9/2009

ISBN: 978-1-4389-6975-6 (sc)

Library of Congress Control Number: 2009902843

Printed in the United States of America
Bloomington, Indiana

This book is printed on acid-free paper.

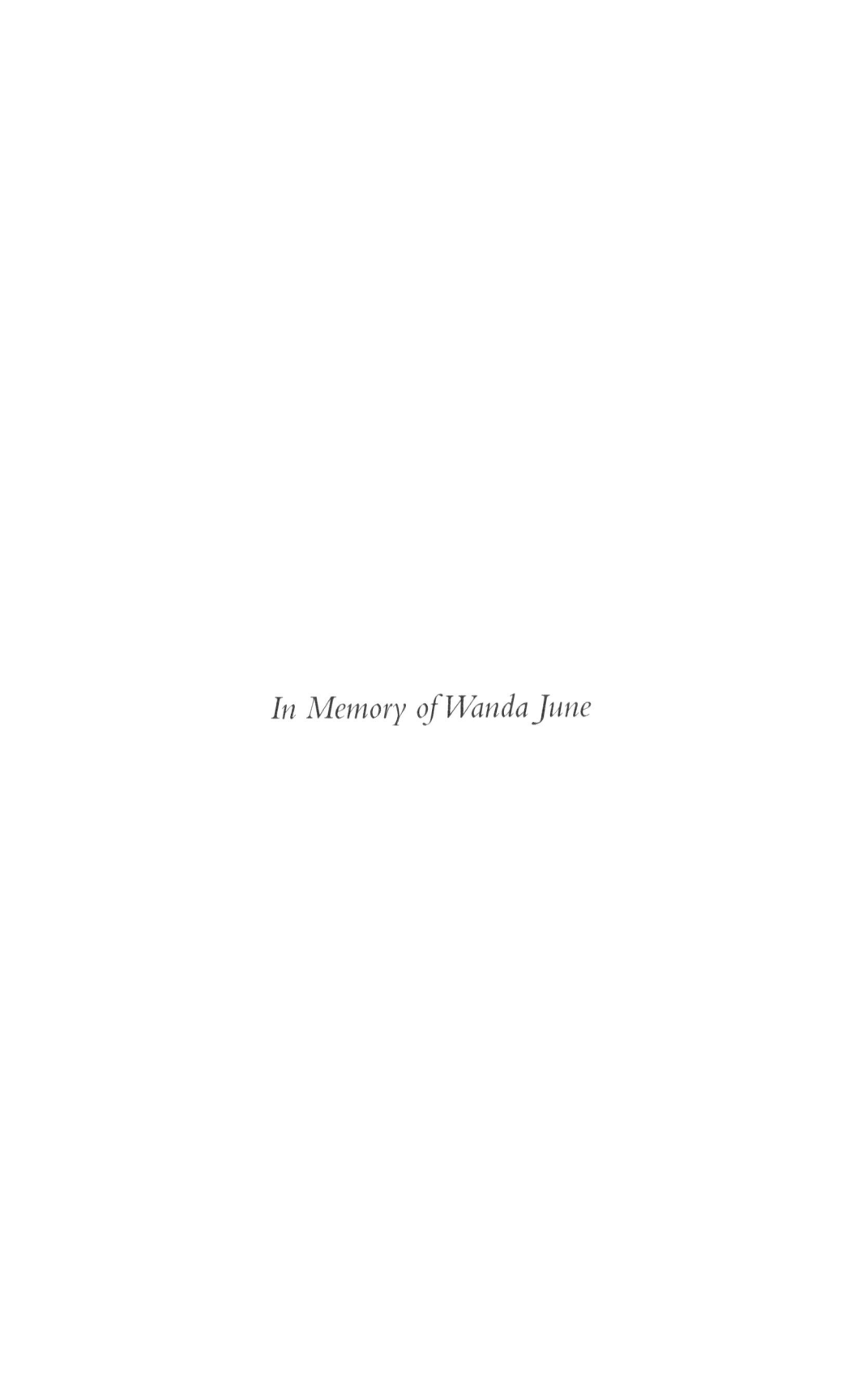

In Memory of Wanda June

This is dedicated to my wife and son, who put up with me everyday and to Stevie for all her hard work.

THE LOST YEARS

"You're never lost until you're found" Vizzuso

The day my life changed seems like forever ago, yet I can remember it like it was just yesterday. My wife gave birth to our new daughter Laken Olivia Vizzuso. My wife, wow, what a person she is. I remember working with her back in the college days at a local fast food establishment. We went out on one date and were married nine months later. She is the perfect partner for a self-absorbed, egotistical maniac like myself.

Jennifer, without a doubt, provides me with warmth, understanding and a firm grip on reality.

Our first child was born in 1990, a son and we named him Zach. It was such a joy holding Zach for the first time and wondering how in the hell I was going to raise a son when I knew nothing about kids. Zach, a spitting image of his old man, was three years old when life became difficult.

Laken was born three years after Zach. I remember her birth and the days that followed very well. The day after her birth I became very ill. I had all the symptoms of the flu. My fever was high with chills and severe aches especially in my neck and head area. I made a trip to the emergency room to make sure everything was ok. They claimed I had the flu and I should go home and rest.

I visited the hospital the next day and smiled when I saw Jennifer holding Laken. She had the beauty of a mother and Laken was an angel. It was two weeks later at home when Laken spiked a fever. In infants fevers in the first month are rare and dangerous. We took Laken to the hospital where she was hospitalized. All tests indicated that she had a slight case of meningitis.

My wife and I took turns staying with her in the hospital as she recovered from this illness. I was beside myself because I had all the classic symptoms of mengititis. In fact, people are misdiagnosed all the time with having the flu. She returned to our home cured several days later.

The night that changed my world seems like an ill-faded nightmare that came to life. Laken, crying for most of the day, had finally fallen asleep on our bed. An upset mother contacted the physician who told her if Laken awoke crying to take her to the emergency room to get checked out. Well, sure enough, she awoke crying and I headed off to the hospital.

The ride to the hospital was no more than fifteen minutes. My wife stayed home with our son Zach as I sped to the hospital. Laken cried more harshly as I drove. I was five minutes from the hospital when the crying stopped. The silence produced the loudest cry of fear I have ever experienced. I quickly turned on the dome light and my heart sunk into a pit of despair as I saw my two month old dead in the car seat. I cannot explain how I felt at that moment. My skin tingles as I write as the emotions are still laced in my memory. Most people cannot fathom the senses in one's body when you witness the death of your child. I remember screaming her name several times as I pulled her out of the car seat and started CPR as I drove.

I ran into the emergency room continuing to administer CPR as I handed her to the nurse. I can tell you at this moment I was beside myself with fear and unguided grief.

I then called my wife to come to the hospital, and together we awaited the outcome.

They had my wife and I sit and wait in a small office with the door closed. My wife, having no medical training or knowledge, was somewhat naïve relative to the situation.

We waited anxiously. I knew if the doctor came in and closed the door our worst fear would be realized. The doctor came in with a nurse and the door did close behind them.

He provided us with the untimely news that our daughter was no longer with us. They tried everything to save her, but all had failed. With this moment followed the slow motion theatrics of a sad Shakespearean play. Tears, grief, pain, and anger consumed my wife and I as we sat in this room.

I took the opportunity granted by the emergency room staff to see Laken. I walked into the room and there my daughter lay on a hospital bed. Her skin was as pale as the white sheets covering her delicate body. A tube was sticking out of her small frail mouth, this very tube used to try and resuscitate her lungs. I hated and cursed the tube that would stand out in my dreams for years to come. Her skin was still warm to the touch with small dotted holes where the staff had tried to bring her back. At this moment, my knees grew weak and tears fell uncontrollably onto the bed as I felt my emotions out of control.

The drive home seemed to take forever, even though it was only five miles. We begged for the answer to the question why? I took Jennifer into the house and sat with her as she lay down on the couch and cried herself to sleep. I then walked into the master bathroom, kneeled down beside the tub and cried until the tears were all gone; morning came.

The morning after was as traumatic as the event itself. My deep rooted guilt started its infancy on many levels. First, I believe that I gave her the first round of germs that eventually caused her death. Secondly, I was a health care worker, how could I not save my little girl? I couldn't help but wonder if I was dreaming a nightmare instead of living it.

My Wife and I made the funeral arrangements. These arrangements were very difficult to maneuver because several family members felt we needed to have full blown calling services. The day after we were challenged by one family member about our decisions. I love this lady today but on that day I made it very clear it was not her decision. The arrangements were to be simple and private.

When my father passed away I found the viewing of his body for the first time very hard. I could not imagine what this viewing would do. Jen and I walked up to the small infant casket. Laken was wrapped in a small blue blanket. Her soft face hardened by the cruel fate of death. I watched as Jennifer kissed her forehead as we both cried.

We went to the grave site and buried our daughter that day. I walked away hugging my brother who had troubled me through my younger years. I fell in his arms crying trying to understand why..

The day after the funeral, we went into Laken's room and removed all items that were a reflection of a new baby. Once again, our tears rang loud as we took down the entire room. The days soon turned into weeks as we attempted to gather our lives back together again. Little did we know our lives would be changed forever.

I represent your typical male personality – one who provides a life for his family, making sure of financial security and holding tight to emotional toughness. I grew up in a modest home with a wonderful family. My father, may he rest in peace, was a ninth grade ethnic drop out who worked 35 years to support his family, only to die eight months following retirement. My mother was the true strength of our household. She had a razor-like mind, mixed with a touch of humor.

I was taught strong values of family, dedication and strength. I, in turn, transferred these attributes to my own family. I graduated from college as a radiology technologist. I was working as an afternoon supervisor in a local hospital when the opportunity to develop and be a proprietor to my own portable x-ray company presented itself. I was in the midst of selling the company when Laken passed away.

I took hold of my strength position after this sad event. I had to portray the strong, realistic voice to provide that special guiding light that would get my family through the tough years. I took all the sadness and emotions and buried them deep within my soul. I had to be the strong one and nothing was going to change my focus.

My wife, on the other hand, needed to grieve normally. I remember the days and months that followed and coming home to tears still flowing as if it had just happened all over again. Her depressed state grew with time, with slated anger fits at other couples with newborn children. Jennifer fell into a never-ending abyss of grief, pain and anger.

My wife changed forever following the death of Laken. It was as though I woke up one morning to a different person.

My overall guilt continued to build. I fully blamed myself for this situation. I had convinced myself that if I would have just stayed home she would be fifteen years old in 2009. The more it grew the harder I worked to suppress my grief. I grew angrier every day. I would wake up in the morning and tell myself to take the first step out of bed and breath. I was hoping that each step would come easier throughout the day.

Her health suffered with horrible migraine headaches to severe female anatomy problems. Her mental and emotional condition continued to weaken. She started looking to me to hold her up and she began to try and find happiness through my actions. The months rolled on and our relationship began to crumble. I, being the macho man, dove into my work more and more everyday to hide from the cruel realities of my life as my wife sunk further and further into a black hole of depression.

Our communication skills fell silent on each other's ears. It is very difficult to communicate with your spouse when you have no idea who you're living with. My son suffered through his own emotions. He would ask perfect strangers if they new his baby sister was dead. Zach went from being potty trained back to diapers. He also noticed that his parents were struggling through these emotional times.

I remember staying at work to get away from going home. The resentment of my wife's lack of strength and my guilt of causing Laken's death ate at me every waking moment and into my nightmares. I could not believe that I could not save her and I was losing my family, my life and my soul. The emotions that I had suppressed for so long started to build to uncontrollable levels. I kept my strength by reinforcing the point of not giving up, which would suppress this ill feeling.

As the days wore on, I began to entertain thoughts of ending this life I was living.

I would look into the eyes of the person I loved only to close them and go somewhere else. I remember telling her the fateful words that I didn't care if she cried anymore.

These words tore through her and damaged her inner feelings. I expressed my disregard for our life as we knew it and created total despair.

Thoughts of my son kept racing through my mind. How could I let him down like

I let his sister down, his mother down and finally myself? He would come up to me and smile and laugh with no worries in the world, yet I planned to hurt him forever by leaving this life. How would he grow up without a stable family?

One momentous night came with a dark cloud. It came as any other night, another serious discussion developed with Jennifer. I was at my breaking point, both mentally and physically. I looked at her and told her that I was going to move out and try to get my life back on track. I knew deep down inside that I would never come back if I left. This particular conversation hit Jennifer hard. I was about ready to call a friend when my pager went off. I had sold my company, but still managed the business. I was on call this night to take care of any emergency x-ray situations. A patient needed a stat hip x-ray in a nursing home 45 minutes away. I hung up the phone and told my wife we would work out the details when I returned.

Leadership; I dare any scholar to actually explain what it is. I thought I was a leader of my employees and my family, but in truth, I knew nothing of true leadership or how it could actually make the difference in any individual's life. I know you want to know what happened to Jennifer and me. Well you will just have to wait until I get done making you aware of your weaknesses, strengths, attributes and faults. This book is geared to expel all myths about leadership. It will provide you with a set path to transform you from a detailed manager to an inspiring leader. Life is measured in the differences we make for others. I have to ask the compelling question:

What differences have you made lately?

A CHOICE: LEADERSHIP

*"A decision is made by the mind –
a choice is made by the heart" Vizzuso*

Well if you are reading this line, then you must have chosen to read on.

Leadership is a choice. Many professors and scholars may disagree with that idea, but I would challenge them to argue the point. I looked up several definitions of leadership and they all make me laugh. I wonder who in the world wrote these prototypical, educational definitions. Surely not people who actually know what leadership is.

Leadership is the art of making the difference for an individual in business, home, school and in friendship. It allows a group of people to come together under one common direction to meet or exceed a goal. It produces strength, endurance and humility in people. It creates a foundation of human relationships that provide awareness not only of one's own self, but awareness of others' inner workings.

I've identified five key components or traits of leadership:

SELF MOTIVATION

A leader must be self-motivated. He or she must have a dedication level far above the norm. The leader must provide a direct motivational tie to his/her employees.

A leader must be willing to work the extra hours both on the job and at home. He/she must be a good model for people. The true leader cares not for the self but for the whole and is demonstrated in all actions. Many will fail to reach the apex of a leaders's height because they are too short on self motivation.

EMPATHY

A leader must care for the people that surround the environment. A good leader will care why an individual is in a bad mood, why another was having personal problems or just plain care about the individual. Leaders have to bring a certain amount of emotion to the art of leadership. I don't mean yelling at everybody for problems that occur, but they must show not only that they can feel, but they can hurt . A leader needs to be willing to join people in their plight and not shy away from emotional connectivity.

PERCEPTIVE REASONING

Perceptive reasoning is the process of identifying critical problems in operational tasks, interpersonal interaction and client-employee interaction and fixing the problems effectively. A leader must adhere to the following steps to achieve this:

- Identify the problem
- Research the problem and determine a temporary fix
- Address critical issues and people
- Provide a logical solution to the problem
- Solve it

For example, an employee comes to me and is upset; I take a break from doing whatever it is I am doing and close my office door to listen to the employee. The employee is upset because she was yelled at by a client about a turn-around-time issue.

She was upset at the day shift person for putting off the work. I listened and understood her frustration. I told her I would take care of the problem. My next move was to start from the beginning and research the problem, and to remember what assumption is to me.

My fact-finding trip led me to the dispatcher, who was responsible for not giving the x- ray call to the day shift employee. I then talked to the dispatcher and explained the implications of communication and how this hurt our service. I showed the dispatcher how to be more effective. I then called the original employee who was upset and explained the entire story. This, in turn, showed her that I followed up, identified the problem, addressed it and solved it. My last call would be to the client to express my concern and explain what happened. This chain of events define perceptive reasoning.

COGNITIVE WISDOM

A leader must be wise in the ways of speaking and making people see differently on common topics. They should realize from a single conversation that a leader knows what is real and what is not. For instance, I developed an in-service on customer service and competition. In the beginning of this in-service, I state where the company is and where we can go. I gave them two options:

- We could sit back, relax and really give up. Then we lose our business, our employment, our respect and we fail.
- We can give it everything we have and strive to be the best.
-

I then stated the following:

"If we give it all and hold nothing back, we are going to be ok. When the smoke clears in t*he end we will be standing together arm in arm, not the company, but us. If we do have failures along the way, then we fail without excuses, without fear of failing and we can live with that and have respect for ourselves.*"

This speech shows the employees that collectively and outwardly I have an outlook, which is somewhat revolutionary. It revealed a line of thinking that was not known to them and projects me in the leadership front seat.

UNDYING RESOLVE

Leadership is a funny quality; it cannot be learned by environmental cues. Either you have it or you don't. Many managers do not and they struggle in their work. The managers who awaken in their roles develop a sense of euphoria within themselves.

When it comes to managing and leading, it is as though you are in a spiritual plane of existence. I, myself one day after a very inspirational speech felt different. I realized that the words I was speaking were not just words but reflections of myself to everyone. I felt higher than the highest clouds and the problems of the region were small and definitely easily defeated. I felt nothing was impossible as long as I lead the way.

This feeling was like a bright light engulfing my mind. I remember sitting one night and believing that I was blessed and my eyes are wide open. This type of feeling I call, *"Leadership Awareness"* and it basically says that you now realize that you are the key to success for your particular company and now you have the vision to accomplish anything you set your mind to.

The big question that I have always asked myself: Can people be managers and not be leaders, yet be successful? The answer to this questions lies in how one defines success. If you define success as a person who works eight hours a day and has a standing job at a company for a period of time, then my answer is yes.

If your definition is like mine and success means rising to the top, achieving all one's goals, having ideological thoughts and being an expert in inspiration, then I would say that you cannot have success without leadership.

I have to say that there are millions of managers and few leaders in the business world. I had the undue pleasure of working with a man that demonstrated what I call the

"Laddership." Laddership is the art of climbing the corporate ladder at any cost, especially the cost of your followers. I remember as a kid watching superman cartoons and there being a villain that was superman's opposite from another universe called the Bizzaro world. This villain was the exact opposite of superman and formed an evil to destroy him. Laddership is the villain of leadership – it represents everything wrong about a person. It allows a person to use unethical means for personal gain. It provides common traits such as:

- Deception
- Cruel behavior
- High self worth
- High controlling tendencies
- Materialism
- Lack of care for others
- Dishonesty

Do the above traits sound like somebody you knew in the past? Well my experience was with a Laddership Master. Jim had just relocated to my region from a state in the Southwest. My current boss was fired for having an unsolicited affair with an employee. Jim had never done operations before in his life. In fact, Jim was primarily a marketing director. He came in with grand words of commitment, leadership and an awareness to take us to the next level. These were all deceptions from a "Ladder". A ladder can provide a smoke screen to cover many weaknesses, but a Ladder's identity is always given away by his or her own actions. Jim systematically let people go, provided no understanding of the business, made horrible decisions such as forging contracts, stealing money from the company and totally demoralizing over 150 employees in a span of one year. Ladders are only in a management position for one reason: self-interest.

Jim's only interest was to make as much money as possible and he wanted an image for our corporate offices to see.

A ladder can ruin lives and can devastate companies. In my case, Jim did not ruin my life, but opened my eyes to what Laddership was and what true leadership meant. I left many friends and colleagues behind when I made the decision to move on in my career. I will forever remember them and their fight to regain a measure of self- respect against the Ladder of all time.

So I have to ask the question, are you a leader or a ladder? If you have to take a few moments to think about your answer, you've already answered the question. You can be a manager and not a leader. This is a very common perspective that many people follow. I've known some really good managers in my time and they do get the job done.

There are many differences between managers and leaders. I've compiled a list of differences that may compel you to rethink who you really are.

Again, Jim cannot have true success in his management role. Jim's success is gauged on his own personal perception. In other words, he is more concerned about image than the company or the employees who work the front line jobs. Jim also is not a risk taker. He fears the repercussions, so he hides from the critical decisions. The other major thing related to leadership that Jim has is a very difficult time with the conceited persona. Jim basically thinks he is way above everyone and he believes he has everybody's respect. Unbeknownst to Jim, you must first respect to gain respect.

Unfortunately for Jim, he has lost this concept at some point in his career.

You will be perceived one of three ways from your peers, loved ones and followers:

DISLIKED, BUT RESPECTED

This scenario can be productive. The manager has the respect of the staff so that he or she can still lead.

LIKED AND RESPECTED

This is the supreme goal a leader should want to achieve. This gives the leader a perfect basis to be very successful and lead employees in the right direction.

DISLIKED AND NOT RESPECTED

This is the worst scenario for any manager. If a leader is disliked and not respected, then he or she will not be able to bring the group together to provide any sort of leadership.

"Fail to honor people, they fail to honor you. But of a good leader, who talks little, when his work is done, his aim fulfilled, they will all say, we did this ourselves."

Lao Tzu

I've basically given you my definition of what leadership is. Do you fit this mold? Do others feel you fit this mold? Many people feel that they have leadership qualities when in reality they are just good managers. This book will challenge you to take an in-depth look at who you really are. It is your choice to accept your results or change them. I will give insights as to why my Libratic Leadership Model provides the best way to build a person from a manager to a leader. My words alone cannot make the difference you need. It will have you looking deep within your own soul and change the key essential traits to become a leader that people will aspire to be and thrive to follow.

If you're ready to turn the next page, welcome to the journey to leadership. It is here you will find out how I made it out of the dark times. If you feel you are already a leader or you are a thriving Ladder and you are happy with that, please close this book and give it to somebody who could truly benefit from it.

Libratic Leadership Model: A Model for Life

"All men dream, but not equally."

"Those who dream by night in the dusty recesses of their minds, awake to find that it was vanity; but the dreamers of the day are dangerous men, that they may act their dreams with open eyes to make it possible." R. Frost.

I walked onto Continental Flight #1997 headed for the fine state of Texas for meetings and visits with both Imaging Centers owned by King's Medical Company. I walked on the crowded flight knowing how tired I was going to be after this week long trip. The day before had been horrible and actually made me physically ill at times. If something could go wrong, it did; from forgetting equipment, to work, to employees forgetting to show up for work. I found my comfortable seat, 13C, and prepared to rest for the short two-hour flight.

The plane took off on time, as usual, one hour late. I rested the reclining seat back and felt mentally and physically exhausted, not realizing I would soon develop pneumonia. My mind still raced about my job: past, present and future. I couldn't continue to be everywhere, anytime and survive the ordeal. The answers to my questions floated eloquently in my mind, but none too clear to grasp. As my mind attempted to shut down, I was interrupted by the conversation of two men who were sitting beside me. I find it a challenge to close my eyes on a plane and listen to other passengers talk, picture their lives and then try and describe to myself what type of person they are. These two men worked at the same company. The older gentleman's name was Bob and the younger, Mike. Bob was Mike's boss and mentor.

Bob and Mike were on a trip to handle some operational problems, which meant disciplining an employee and possibly terminating that same employee. They were also going to meet with the rest of the staff and go over goals and operational issues; they would be handling some customer complaints and problems.

Mike was very unsure of how to handle these types of issues. All through the conversation, Mike would repeat the same words, *"How do you think we should do this?"* Bob was very confident in his sentence structures and choice of words and told Mike the following passage:

"Mike, you'll be fine. I'll step back and let you handle this situation, which will give you the experience that you need. I'll just give you moral support and back you up. You watch, everything will work out just fine."

I heard these words and had what literary geniuses call an "Epitaph" or an awakening moment. The answers that plagued me came in a rush.

I read books all the time on leadership, management and success in business.

These books give theories, principles, definitions and scientific jargon; but they all lack one thing and Bob lacks that same thing as a manager. All these books and most managers lack the ability to systematically instruct someone on how to be an effective leader and manager within their given environment.

I, too, fell into this pitfall of management. I was not instructing managers to manage, but to follow me into the light. I provided the managers and marketing representatives with training classes last year, but failed to truly teach any technique. I left each person the duty of self-learning. I just went through two years of self-learning to acquire my masters degree and discovered self-learning is awful.

The **Libratic Leadership Management Model** is a new, non-traditional method of leadership. This model allows an individual to explore one's own self; to unleash a freedom seldom realized by leaders and managers. This is not just a model to be lectured about nor is it to be tucked away on a bookshelf somewhere, but an actual twelve-month program designed to actually teach progressive management and leadership practices.

It will actually allow an individual to become totally formless in their leadership and management styles. It will improve weaknesses and highlight strengths. It provides an overall strategy to increase skills, while decreasing inefficiencies by removing strict lines of classification and inflexibility.

Libratic Leadership Model Defined

The word "Libratic" is derived from the Spanish word "libre" meaning; free without confinement. Libratic Leadership Model is defined as a formless approach to leadership and management skills. It provides the ability to take advantage of all the positive qualities of current styles of leadership and management models. It provides a platform for a person to conform to any situation and produce successful outcomes.

The center of the model is one's inner self. This model provides the opportunity to:

- Improve weaknesses
- Exploit strengths
- Increase adaptability
- Increase problem solving skills
- Improve interpersonal relationship building
- Decrease employee turnover
- Improve overall performance

There are nine distinct parts to the Libratic Leadership Management Model:

- Self
- Communication
- Relationship
- Attitude
- External Life
- Character
- Action
- Management
- Financial Awareness

Leadership/Management Models

There are three common leadership/management models:

- Autocratic
- Laissez-faire
- Democratic

Autocratic

There are many autocratic type leaders and managers in the work place. This model demonstrates an authoritative base surrounded by sound judgement and control.

An authoritative leader/manager has three distinct traits to their internal make-up:

- Controller
- General
- Student

Controller

The controller is the attribute that provides control over aspects of the business and employees. It provides safety and improved self-esteem for this type of leader. It allows for an individual to focus on controlling elements of success such as:

- Decreased expenditure
- Increased profitability
- Improved planning
- Proactive problem solving

- Improved quality

This allows a person to break apart normal situations into small refined elements to provide extreme detailed management. The controller exhibits control over employees to extreme measures. Employees are not permitted to free think or demonstrate free will.

In fact, all actions or reactions are controlled to predict outcomes.

In theory, the controller represents the intelligence of the autocratic leader.

However, in many situations the controller is more of a protective layer of behavior. In fact, in extreme cases, can make a person cruel and inhumane in order to protect personal and professional interests. This is called Control Anxiety and can typically provide the following results:

- Increased employee turnover
- Reduction in success
- Increased stress levels
- Loss of market share
- Decreased profitability
- Termination

The general provides strategic planning and goal setting for the autocratic leader.

It provides:

- Logical thinking
- Goal setting
- Organizational skills
- Long-term thinking
- Ambition
- Achievement
- Problem solving

The general allows an individual to create plans and achieve goals. It creates the vision that the controller needs to accomplish. It allows for creative thinking and flexibility. The general is the distinct leadership part to the autocratic leader. It creates vision, purpose and success. It also provides the opportunity to create strong loyalties from the people who follow. The general's vision and purpose must be aligned with the followers to create harmony.

In most cases, the general does demand loyalty and respect from the other people; the true challenge is keeping it. In many cases, autocratic leaders have loyalty in the beginning, but lose it along the way due to Control Anxiety. The subjects lose interest in the vision because of poor treatment and/or increased failure and loss, which makes the person leave or attempt to dethrone the autocratic leader.

A weak, non-focused general will cause Morale Deprivation and Focus

Deficiency Syndrome. Morale Deprivation is the process by which the overall morale of the followers are systemically taken away because of poor leadership actions. It produces multiple problems for the autocratic leader such as:

- Low customer service
- Poor employee performance
- Low loyalty
- High employee turnover
-

Focus Deficiency Syndrome is a very common problem in the art of leadership. It occurs when a leader loses focus on key elements to become successful. A leader may focus on incorrect aspects of a situation. A leader may also have an overall lack of focus on particular steps or details that are vastly important to a successful outcome. An autocratic leader has specific problems with this because the controller may focus on the wrong elements, thus creating negative controls, which may lead to failures.

"Focus Determines Reality"

Student

The student is the knowledge seeker in an autocratic leader. Autocratic leaders have a certain thirst to gain as much knowledge as possible. This thirst drives the student to acquire knowledge in many different ways:

- Education system
- Internship
- Gossip trails
- Self study
- Life experience
- Forceful extraction

This knowledge feeds both the controller and the general to support their needs for control and vision. However, a person may express what is termed, Self-

Actualization Complex. Self-Actualization Complex is defined as the process by which a person believes he/she knows more than they actually do. A leader may feel that he/she knows all there is to know, and in fact stops providing the other parts of necessary information needed to maintain successful outcomes.

I currently work with a very autocratic peer. Betty is very intense and very demanding of her people. I watch her in senior leadership meetings display her empowerment. She removed many mid level managers when she joined the organization. Autocratic leaders tend to surround themselves with hand chosen people who support their philosophy and who are easily controlled.

As a peer my relationship with Betty is very strong. I actually learn from her style, taking away what I need. I've been very impressed by her composer and aggression. However, I wonder if she continues to succeed in the wake of change. One thing is for certain I would definitely be cheering for her.

A True Autocratic: Genghis Khan

The Mongols nomadic warriors of Central Asia were united under Temujin (Genghis Khan) in the thirteenth century. He conquered most of Asia, parts of Europe and the Middle East. The Mongols principal tool was speed in all things, on or off the battlefield. The Mongols were masters of organization, discipline, communication, and rapid decision-making. Their system lasted several centuries, telling you that there was more to it than a temporary military advantage. The myths coming down to us portray the Mongols as a bunch of wild, undisciplined barbarians. This is utterly false, for the Mongols did what they did using world-class management techniques.

Genghis Khan was born into a family of noble background. His father was killed when he was a child and his family lived on the run from rival tribes. When Temujin grew of age he had several items he wanted to accomplish.

- He wanted to take back his family position.
- He wanted to realize the yearning of all Mongols for as long as anyone could remember, he wanted to conquer the world.
- He first gained control over his own tribe, starting with over 1,000 followers and was faced with competition from over half a million hostile Mongols. Temujin applied a ruthlessness his follow Mongols could understand and appreciate. His goal was to take the tribe further than ever before and make all his followers rich.

In 1185 Temujin became Khan (king) of his tribe. Over the next ten years he conquered and/or absorbed all the Mongol tribes. In 1206, the Mongols proclaimed him as Genghis Khan (supreme king). He then invaded China to conquer over 100 million people. No Central Asian tribe had ever conquered China and for Temujin, it would take over two generations. He laid down the foundation for a system that was able to keep subjection going for another two centuries of conquest.

The following items set Temujin apart from other leaders:

Incentives

Temujin was one of the first leaders to actively use incentives to motivate his troops. He would take over a tribe and reward his troops with wealth, women and property. He would also use "life" as a natural incentive. When Temujin came upon a new tribe or city, the standard offer was complete instant surrender, or total obliteration.

Entire cities and tribes were killed when they resisted. All men, women, children and animals were killed and the cities were burned to the ground. The incentives increased motivation and loyalty to Temujin.

Loyalty

Temujin was able to create loyalty to himself and his officers that went beyond the tribe and family. He further weakened tribal loyalties by mixing warriors from several different tribes. The absorption of non-Mongol tribes would provide a relative neutral mix to his followers. The addition of incentives even further increased the loyalties.

Discipline

Mongol combat methods were adapted from techniques used in hunting. Mongols depended on hunting for much of their food and hunting was considered serious business.

When strict discipline was taken for granted, the leader of the hunt could enforce obedience with harsh punishments. Temujin institutionalized the traditional Mongol discipline throughout his entire army. Executing a few errant troopers on the spot usually inspired others no matter what nationality they were.

Political Cunning

Temujin was, above all, an astute politician. Temujin uncovered internal disagreements among his enemies and would deal with the contending parties to weaken his opponents before gaining their allegiance or destroying them. He could deal with a foreign country from a position of strength because of his "join or die" policy.

Speed

The most remarkable asset Temujin possessed was his use of speed in all things.

He moved fast because he wanted to conquer all before he grew old and there was a tactical advantage against his enemies. Speed was life when hunting, and he transferred this into his method of leadership. Speed was the difference between success and failure.

Organization

Temijun tinkered with organization and made sure it was standard in all Mongol armies. This made it easy to train troops and officers. It also allowed for the same tactical operations throughout the entire army.

Knowledge and Communication

Collecting information and then getting training and information to the commanders were crucial to Temujin's success. His intelligence system included spies, scholars and far-ranging scouts. The communication set-up was remarkable for the time.

The 19th century pony express was very similar. The Mongols would establish remote stations at 50 mile intervals. The messengers would stop at each site to rest, get food and get a fresh horse. They would commonly toot a horn before arriving at a station, a fresh horse and saddle would be ready and waiting. A messenger could travel up to 200 miles in one day.

People Skills

Temujin knew how to deal with people. He was able to choose his friends and enemies very carefully. His own father was poisoned by a friend. His real skill was dealing with the so called "civilized world." Many of the countries to the south surrendered quickly to the Mongols and Temujin had to choose wisely on whom they could trust. It was essential to select effective and reliable administrators. He used these same skills to hire non-Mongol commanders. He couldn't afford to use Mongols only, because his army would not have enough troops.

Ruthlessness

One must realize that Temujin's success was based on his ruthlessness. In fact, the Mongols killed 12% of the world's population. This compares to Hitler, who in the

1940's killed 4% of the world's population. The Mongols were three times as murderous as Germany in World War II. He was focused on acquiring his goals and would not flinch in his practices.

Adaptability

A crucial aspect of Temujin's personality was his ability to adapt. The Mongols overcame their nomadic preferences and learned how to adapt to the ways of farmers and city dwellers.

Laissez-Faire

The laissez-faire leader is the true people's champion. He/she becomes successful by using interpersonal skills combined with management techniques to produce positive outcomes. The laissez-faire leader has three distinct characteristics to their internal make-up:

- Mentor
- Manager
- Friend

Mentor

The mentor is the element that provides leadership and guidance to the followers.

It provides an avenue for growth for the leader and the followers. The laissez-faire manager thrives on coaching and interpersonal development. This allows for success in the following areas:

- Employee growth
- Low employee turnover
- Improved productivity

The mentor seeks knowledge for the benefit of all surrounding people. The knowledge makes the mentor feel a high degree of confidence. However, there are times when the mentor may seek and find knowledge, but then never use that knowledge. This is called Knowledge Block. Knowledge Block occurs quite often because the mentor may lack the skills to use it.

The mentor is generally very ethical in the delivery of supervision and overall business practices. The individual is very honest and up front with customers, employees and upper management. This honesty provides a basis for open communication and active listening.

Manager

The manager provides basic operational duties, while providing organizational structure and proactive problem solving. There are times when weak laissez-faire managers lack organizational skills due to lack of management experience, called Disorganizational Behavior. This type of behavior is an effect that allows an individual to be very disorganized, which may lead to:

- Missed deadlines
- Low control measurements
- Decreased profitability

The manager handles all aspects of management, providing communication, direction, problem solving, implementation of policies and procedures, human resource management, financial budgeting and goal setting. Unfortunately, these duties may range from aggressive to passive in a laissez-faire leader. Passive Attrition provides a low level of management strength.

It allows for severe problems to occur in the overall leadership structure. It produces outcomes such as:

- Lack of respect

- Decreased profitability
- Morale Deprivation
- Employee resentment
- Poor problem solving
- Poor quality of performance
- Decreased Longevity

Friend

The friend represents the interpersonal relationship building function of the laissez-faire leader. The laissez-faire leader can build strong relationships between employees, customers and administration. These relationship-building skills provide a bond between the leader and the follower, and allows the relationship to produce positive outcomes such as:

- Increased employee satisfaction
- Increased loyalty
- Improved customer service and marketability

There are several major pitfalls associated with the friend that will make the difference between success and failure for a laissez-faire leader. Discipline Deficiency is the problem that many weak laissez-faire leaders contend with on a day-to-day basis.

The individual relies on friendship more than common sense to handle problems with employees. In fact, the laissez-faire leader loses the ability to discipline an employee.

This loss will destroy all management capabilities and lead to failure.

It also allows the Negative Catalyst to develop and mature. A Negative Catalyst is a person that attacks a leader for personal and professional reasons. This person uses any tool to complete the attack. The Negative Catalyst will sway other employees to question the leader in all that they do and try to create false realities to higher levels of administration. The ultimate goal is to eliminate the laissez-faire leader to try and gain power. Weak laissez-faire leaders cannot survive an attack from a negative catalyst. In comparison, the autocratic leader would be able to identify this type of person and find a way either to control the situation or remove the particular person.

The laissez-faire leader provides these three distinct parts into one persona. This persona may have both positive and negative outcomes depending on the severity of problematic behaviors.

Karen is a very dear friend of mine. She just happens to be the most laissez faire person I know. She is challenged with leading a group of people that are highly specialized. Karen has a hard time separating herself from the line workers. This on one hand creates very strong interpersonal relationships but almost makes her a non-factor in leading the team. Karen struggles with this day in and day out and it will be her fate one day.

The People's Champion: Frederick The Great

A generation before the American Revolution, Frederick The Great, the king of Prussia, lost as many battles as he won, but did so with far fewer resources than his opponents. Frederick entered the high stakes game of war and international politics with the deck heavily stacked against him. Yet Frederick prevailed, and not because of luck or divine intervention. The lessons he learned, applied and built upon are still valid.

Frederick was known as The Great not because he conquered Europe, or even a large part of it, but because he was able to survive while being surrounded by powerful enemies and he was close to his followers. Frederick was able to take smaller resources and leverage them in order to become successful.

Frederick started to understand his role in society at the young age of one. His father had expanded the country through peaceful terms while increasing the size of the army. However, he did leave Frederick a lot of debt to handle. Frederick would expand his borders by invading Silesia and would build his army to last through the Seven Years'

War (1756-63), which was an attempt to destroy Prussia by the Austrian Empire and its allies.

Frederick despised the French lifestyle that his father had created. He soon dismantled the French-style court system. The new King lived more like a town mayor than a monarch. The army continued to grow under Frederick. In fact, many of the soldiers were foreign recruits. This made him look exceptional because his own people did not have to take up arms.

One of his greatest challenges was being "The Enlightened Prince." This was the humanist philosophy his grandfather had practiced. A key aspect of this was the concept that a monarch served his subjects. He actually authored a book titled, "Anti-Machiavellian", which describes how a leader should act and criticizes the earlier book titled, The Prince by Machiavel.

Fortunately for Frederick, he had a wealth of talent and techniques available to meet the challenges he faced throughout his career, such as:

Recognizing Opportunity

Frederick knew an opportunity when he saw one and rarely let one go or unused.

Shortly after he became King, the Holy Roman Empire's king died without an heir. His daughter wanted the throne for herself and took it. She was stuck with an army that was worn out from years of war. The rest of Europe was fighting each other and paid no attention to the new ruler. Frederick sensed an opportunity to add the province of Silesia.

The new queen governed Silesia. He could not take it just because he felt like it, because he was practicing the enlightened prince philosophy. He found a way to take the land by force, due to the fact that it offered a threat to his current state. He then invaded and captured the territory.

Personal Leadership and Respect for Subordinates

Frederick's troops were also very motivated. This was mainly due to Frederick's own personal leadership. Most kings of the time did not lead their armies into battle, but

Frederick did. He shared the battlefield with his troops. He was very familiar with his troops and would joke around with them. He believed that all men were equal and always stayed around the troops during a campaign. He would share the credit for victories with his men, which solidified their loyalty.

Mentors and Personal Training

Because of his father, Frederick's education was complete. When he took over the throne, he separated from his father and started to study as much as possible. He would also surround himself with men who were also learning and had great talent. He would then become a mentor himself to his Generals.

Finding Good Men and Keeping Them

Frederick knew in order to win battles he needed the best Generals available. He would use aristocrats and professional soldiers for his officer core. He would offer them twice the money any other kingdom would pay. In order to keep these good officers he would promote them as fast as possible.

Leisure

Frederick knew the importance of leisure. If a leader was always working, he would burn out or, at the very least, become sour. He would take time off and relax and he made his officers do the same.

Training

The Prussian Army had intensive training. To defeat the larger forces they had to react faster and perform all maneuvers to perfection. In fact, the troops had a high tendency to die during the training. Frederick wrote instruction manuals for both infantry and cavalry operations.

Outsourcing

In order to have a large standing army, Frederick would purchase the services of mercenaries to strengthen his weaknesses. He recognized that he needed all the help available.

Innovation

The greatest challenges Frederick faced were being outnumbered on the battlefield by horse artillery, and thinning the ranks of his soldiers to increase muzzle- reloading time. These innovations provided him with a tactical advantage.

Democratic

The democratic leader, otherwise known as The Leader of Delegation, is the most popular means of leadership. It provides people with a leader that portrays everything that is good and honest in the world. The democratic leader, however, can suffer severe problems due to underlying tendencies. A quality democratic leader will provide the following qualities:

- Increased communication
- Improved employee morale
- Positive results
- Employee growth

The democratic leader possesses three distinct parts:

- Facilitator
- Delegator
- Protector

Facilitator

The democratic leader's strongest character is the facilitator. The facilitator is the component that provides innovation and that special spark to get things done right the first time. It allows an individual to strategically prepare for the fluent art of business.

The facilitator allows the risk taker role to mature. Risk taking is a key function to any leadership role. It is extremely important for the democratic leader. If the risk factor is too high, the individual may develop Risk Adherence. Risk Adherence is the process where the individual takes miscalculated risks and fails to produce expected outcomes.

Risk avoidance can also occur in a democratic leader. Risk avoidance is an overall decrease in risk taking actions. This provides few business opportunities and increased stagnate business flow that leads to business and personal failures.

The facilitator takes the group of followers and provides a detailed plan of goals to accomplish. The plan is devised to take advantage of all the group's strengths, and limits its weakest points. The facilitator will make sure each distinct part starts on time and moves at an acceptable speed. The facilitator doesn't necessarily actually perform the essential tasks, but guides the group in doing so.

Delegator

The Delegator represents the heart and soul of the democratic leader. The goal of a democratic leader is to provide personal growth to all followers. This is accomplished by using delegation in every aspect of the day-to-day leadership and management techniques. Delegation in its purist form allows for:

- Personal growth
- Decreased stress levels
- Identifies future management prospects
- Increased productivity

The art of delegation isn't an easy thing to master. In fact, it is one of the hardest management aspects. One cannot just hand tasks to a person and expect them to get it done correctly and on time. The

Delegator must provide leadership to the followers to insure they get the delegated tasks done. The one true problem arises when tasks are given without the addition of guidance. Delegation Drift describes the problem when delegation is used without guidance, which produces a negative swing for delegation.

Delegation Drift provides an opportunity for increased errors and failure.

Delegation must be precise and planned. Democratic leaders may use vague plans or instructions that confuse the follower. This is called Wide Delegation. Wide Delegation is a byproduct of lack of detail. An employee or follower must have complete instructions with objectives and goals. If the instructions are too vague, then increase in errors can be expected, which may lead to failure.

Good delegation will improve communication pathways between the leader and the followers. It increases verbal communication and enhances active listening. It allows for nonrestrictive communication airways. It also allows for important input and idea generation. Restrictive communication develops when communication is impaired and ideas and thoughts are suppressed.

Protector

The protector provides loyalty and protection for the followers. The protector acts as the father of the family. It will provide Undying Resolve, which represents the mentality of never giving into fears and obsessions. Employees do not follow titles, but follow courage and integrity. The protector provides the courage to stand up for the entire group in good and bad times.

The democratic leader provides three distinct components into one persona. This persona has both positive and negative outcomes, depending on the severity of problematic behaviors.

Tim was my leader for several years. He was calm, very democratic and fair in his approach. He always took feedback and dwelled heavily on devotion and sacrifice. Tim would at times self reflect himself into a deep somber sleep. He was respected by his peers and looked upon by the workers. Tim's success will be determined by his ability to make or not make a decision. This choice plaques all democratic leaders because their ability to lead is determined by consensus not by authority.

U.S. Grant: The Tycoon of Turnaround

American Civil War General Ulysses S. Grant was not as spectacular a field commander as many of his adversaries, in particular Robert E. Lee, but Grant was adept at rapidly turning around disastrous situations. Grant was the turtle that eventually won the race to victory against rabbits like Lee. Grant never succeeded at non-military business, but in the chaos of war left a legacy of lessons that can still be learned from.

His father was a butcher and young Grant wanted nothing to do with his father's trade. An opportunity came knocking in 1838, when his father came home and declared that Ulysses was going to West Point. Grant did not distinguish himself academically and graduated near the middle of his class in 1843.

Grant served his country in the American Mexican War through 1846. He was promoted twice during this time. The separation from his wife soon became too much and he resigned his commission and moved back home to be with his wife and family.

He was recruited at the beginning of the Civil War to form a company of volunteers from the Galena, Illinois area. His first battle came in the fall of 1861 and the last came in the spring of 1865. He kept getting promoted due to his successes on the battlefield, until he became in charge of the entire Union Army.

Grant faced many challenges through these times. He was instrumental in fighting a war on the battlefields, while also winning the political battles of his politicians. The political battles were as fierce as the Confederate battles. Secondly, he faced the challenge of taking a nonprofessional army and molding the soldiers into an organized, successful force. The following democratic traits helped Grant realize success even to the seat of president.

Clear Communication

An important characteristic of Grant was his communication skills, both written and verbal. Most generals in the Civil War had problems giving clear and precise orders.

Grant would handle most of the communication to his subordinates himself. He told them the important details and was always clear on the final objective of the order.

He was also a very astute active listener. He would listen to his officers which, in turn, helped him understand the elements of battle that he could not foresee. He encouraged feedback from his officers. This was very unusual, in the past, for generals to actively listen to positive or negative comments. Grant took these comments as a true democratic leader would, as knowledge and input.

Optimist

Grant was a great optimist and carried this trait throughout the war. He appeared to be defeated on several occasions, but his optimism and confidence would pull him and his troops through. In one particular battle, the Confederate army had surprised Grant's army while they were camped. The Union Camps had been overrun and the troops were pushed to the limit. An officer asked Grant if he intended to retreat across the river, Grant replied, "No I propose to attack at daylight and whip them." His optimistic attitude set Grant apart from his contemporaries. Where other Generals saw defeat, Grant saw victory and when other Generals saw problems, Grant saw solutions. This was the mark of a natural democratic leader.

Solution Oriented

Grant was solution oriented in his management approach. He felt that problems only existed so solutions could be found, and he mentored his officers to take that same approach. The solution minded subordinates proved to be the difference between success and failure.

Daring

Grant was very aggressive and took risks. This was supported by his confidence and optimistic attitudes. He made daring moves while other Generals would have taken more passive routes. This proved to be very effective in the Civil War.

Calmness

Grant had the uncanny act of remaining calm during horrible times and conditions. His actions would inspire his officers who, in turn, inspired the troops to rally.

Delegation and Trust of Others

Grant used delegation to its fullest extent. He trusted his officers and allowed them to succeed under his command. He would delegate many duties that other Generals would never think to.

Focus and Persistence

Once Grant had a goal, he was determined to reach it at any cost. He was focused and persistent in his leadership.

I just described three great leaders, each providing a different leadership style.

They all became very successful as leaders, yet they all had flaws and problems. The art of Libratic Leadership is the ability to become one of the three leadership models at any moment. In other words, attack like Genghis Khan in one moment and befriend your follower like Frederick The Great the next. The challenge is to change how you think, how you perceive yourself and how daring you are to make the critical difference.

The Libratic Leadership Model is within all of us. It represents the ability to change generations of programmed behaviors and change one's own inner self. The following chapters will address each distinct element of the true leadership model.

Are you ready to change?

SELF

"You cannot know others until you know yourself."

The self is defined as the spark of life that makes up an individual's inner being. It provides person, personality, dislikes, enjoyment, emotional disposition and temperament.

Chi

H20 Principle

Chi is the Chinese word for "self". The perfect Chi illustrates the **H20 Principle** which, in turn, demonstrates the properties of formlessness in the sense of mimicking the natural properties of water. Water, in its natural state, demonstrates the following qualities.

- Water is the softest substance in the world, yet it can break rock.
- Water is the universal solvent substance. It can dissolve rock over time.
- Water can be used as an agent to heal ailments.
- Water can be very powerful and destroy cities with powerful waves of destruction.
- If one pours water into a cup, it becomes the cup. If it is poured into a jug, it becomes the jug.

- Water has no true form or structure, but becomes the environment that surrounds it.

Imagine you were a drop of water that falls to the ground into a small depression in the earth. You adapt instantly to your environment and you become the shape of the depression. Just fantasize for a moment – the ability to become any given leader, at any given time! This would allow you to become an effective leader and overcome all obstacles. It would change the person you seen in the mirror on a daily basis.

Three Types of Chi

There are three general types of Chi:

- External Chi
- Internal Chi
- Pseudo Chi

External Chi

The External Chi is the self that an individual displays to the external environment. It consists of attributes that an individual wants to reveal to the outside world. It constitutes only the parts of a person that an individual chooses to display on a routine basis. For example:

Men do not allow themselves to cry in front of others. Crying is viewed as a sign of weakness and insecurity. It threatens their manly persona, thus is not part of their self that will be revealed.

Internal Chi

The Internal Chi is the self that an individual displays only to close friends and family or is so private, one only shows to himself. It provides the ability to handle stressful or emergency situations by enabling a person's natural instincts of "flight or fight". In times of crisis, the Internal Chi may override the External Chi to provide protection. For example:

Men have difficulties facing the death of a loved one. In these troubled times Internal Chi's generally have little difficulty crying in front of other people.

<u>Pseudo Chi</u>

The Pseudo Chi is the self that an individual creates to hide both the Internal and External Chi. This is done to provide a false presentation and impression. In most cases, the Pseudo Chi is very weak and usually fails to work over long periods of time. For example:

My former manager was a Pseudo Chi and came across as caring about his employees. He was an aggressive leader and he cared about the overall company service. In time, his true Chi revealed itself as a man who cared only about himself and how he looked to everyone else.

Society's Sterotypes: Chi's Challenge

Society has determined that human beings have certain inherited personal traits and personalities. It stresses that these inherited traits determine one's behavior in given situations. The true being can learn some alternatives to their normal behavioral traits, but for the most part react in a constant behavioral pattern. The challenge for an individual is to erase these stereotypical impressions by being able to use each Chi at any given moment in conjunction with each other. This will allow the person to have a formless inner self, to better deal with the stresses of life.

Four Attributes of the Formless Chi

The adaptation of a formless Chi is the ultimate goal in leadership and management. This will provide four primary attributes:

- Passion
- Strength
- Wisdom
- Knowledge

<u>Passion</u>

Passion is a very important factor in a person's life. If one truly wants to succeed in accomplishing a goal, there must be some passion behind the person. The Formless Chi provides that passion to succeed. It provides passion to seek out knowledge and wisdom to ensure that growth is achieved. A truly passionate person can convince even the most skeptical to believe. In fact, passionate people display these emotions in their actions and their facial expressions and especially the burning desire located within their eyes.

Strength

Strength is essential to live life itself. In life, both personal and business, there are times when problems arise and make life awfully hard. The Formless Chi provides strength to weather storms and prevails in the end. Strength is measured in both action and attitude and intertwines with performance, happiness and contentment.

Wisdom

The art of wisdom has been studied and used for thousands of years. It represents the ability to determine truths from non-truths. The Formless Chi develops wisdom in providing solutions to problems that would remain unsolved. It allows a person to make proactive decisions to determine true meanings of life.

Knowledge

Knowledge is described as information processed and reprocessed and used appropriately. The Formless Chi develops a burning desire to seek and understand knowledge. This knowledge and understanding is needed to continue growth for the

Formless Chi. It allows a person to become stronger as the knowledge grows within them. It allows the formless attribute to grow and mature within the inner self.

Adaptability

A leaders has to be totally adaptable in any given situation. This adaptability is the key component to the success of this model. It allows a person to take pieces from all the models. In many cases that person acts as a filter to find the best course to make a difference. This adaptability is not easy to learn or use. Many leaders try and fail through out years of responsibility. The measure of dismay can turn a true leader into a tired manager. Unfortunately the failing aspect is a natural aspect of this model called, Trial by Failure. In each case of failure the leader will adapt and learn thus creating adaptability.

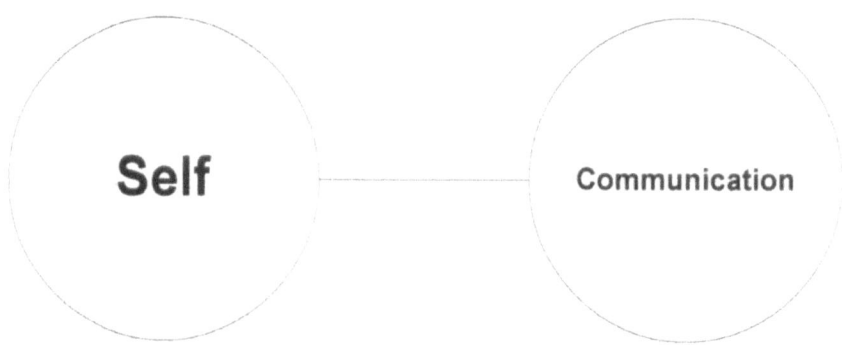

Communication

*"Communication is as important to leadership
as air is to breathing."*

The Three C's of Success

Recently I went to a local bookstore in search of a motivational business book to gain more insight on improving my skills as a manager. I started looking at several different texts and found them not only boring, but also offensive. The average run of the mill book used top ten lists, suggestive lists and mediocre groupings to try and encourage growth in management. This is offensive to the top skilled managers, because those individuals know how to manage. They just want some eye opening examples of past experiences of successful people.

I, on the other hand, will not stoop to this literal low level and bore you to death with a bunch of useless lists that have no value other than use as scrap paper. I have developed three basic perspectives that reveal the true essence of success. These three ideals will provide cognitive perspective to life's greatest challenges.

These ideals are the **THREE C'S OF SUCCESS:**

- COMMUNICATION
- COOPERATION

• CORRELATION

COMMUNICATION

Many dictionaries define communication as the art of transferring data from one source to another through verbal and non-verbal channels. I beg to differ with this cliche' definition. I define communication as:

> *The active cognitive act of delivering certain stimuli in conjunction with receiving this stimuli to produce an effective bond between social, cultural and spiritual essences.*

I cannot agree with the notation that communication is placed on a single plain atmosphere. Many people feel if one does not speak, one does not communicate. This presents the depressing state of our current sociological stature.

> *Communication, without a shadow of doubt, is the single most important thing in any animal's existence. Yes, I mean animal, not just humans. Communication is taken for granted in the business, social and home environments. This concept can actually determine* **life** *and* **death**, **winning** *and* **losing**, **love** *and* **hate** *and* **wealth** *and* **poverty**. *This simple premise can build countries, yet it can destroy them just as fast.*

To my dismay, there are many entities that are horrible at communication, because either they generally do not care or they do not have an effective personality to communicate properly.

Effective leaders must be able to communicate effectively throughout their daily activities. They must not only be able to speak clearly and concisely, but they must be able to use active listening to its highest potential. They must listen to what their customers say they need and not try guessing what they need. It is like going to a restaurant and ordering a meal. You state exactly what you want, and the place of service prepares your meal the way you ordered. When leaders do not listen, it is like entering a restaurant and having the waiter or waitress order your dinner without asking what you want, in turn, you receive something you never wanted. Many people lack empathy towards their customers, which is a direct result of poor listening.

The most critical part of communication is not the verbal cues, but the non-verbal tendencies. This can **directly** affect the entire operation of a small business or a giant corporation. For example, I can recall many days where I thought the world was crashing down. I recall walking into my office in severely foul moods. I hated the world for whatever reason and I displayed this, no I must say "shared" this with my employees.

This had a drastic effect on my employees. My negative attitude directly affected their day. In turn, they negatively affected our customers. I indirectly communicated negative thoughts to my customers in the office.

I then saw the problem for what it was worth. I started performing controlled experiments with my staff to see the objective effects of this **Osmosis Effect** of indirect communication. I found the following facts to be true:

- *My attitude directly affected my entire operation.*
- *The impact of my attitude was greater than my communication.*
- *If I smiled, they smiled even bigger; If I frowned, they frowned more deeply.*
- *Employees will derive their emotions from their manager and/or marketer. Good or bad.*

There are too many managers in the corporate world that have no time for their customers. The employees of a non-communicative manager start a process that I term

MANAGER RESENTMENT. This syndrome starts the first time a manager is perceived as being uncaring or does not take the time to honestly listen to an employee.

The "cancer" has begun and within days every employee feels that the manager has short changed them, even though they have had no negative contact with the manager.

This problem is usually temporary if the manager realizes his or her mistake.

However, if they do not, then the problem will be ongoing and directly affect the operations of the particular unit or company.

The other common problem is called the **CORPORATE MUDSLIDE.** This phenomenon begins at the higher level of management communicating policies and procedures, to the middle management level. The middle management level then takes these communications and delivers them at the employee level. At this time, they may take this message and wrap a negative attitude towards it, which is then perceived as a negative communication. For example:

The corporation mandates that all yearly raises will be going from 5% to 2.5%.

The reason for this decline is to control costs for the future of the company. It is the mind set to give smaller raises now so that the company survives and they can give the raises for a longer period of time.

Middle management hears and understands this premise, but communicates nothing of the reason at the employee level; thus giving a non-communicative interaction that leads them to believe the company does not care. In fact, the company is caring and that is why the decision was made in the first place.

This type of non-communication can severely hurt an established organization and it will kill a company that is small and whose success of the business is dependent on fast growth. It also taints the attitude of not only front level employees, but to middle management.

Many times, as a leader I stressed the seriousness of communication to my staff.

Many times, a simple phone call would make the difference between a happy client and an ex-client.

For example: My mobile x-ray company had just acquired a new client in an area where we could not penetrate. This particular client was having severe service problems with their current provider. The first week went great, then disaster hit me at 11:00 pm. I received a call from the supervisor of the nursing home. This nurse was very upset at the length of turnaround time it was taking to get results of an x-ray. The call had come in at 3:00pm and still there were no results. My stomach felt sour and sickly. I said I would look into it and call her right back. In my mind, I remember the call coming inand the x-ray technologist was on her way to do the exam. What in the world happened? I asked myself. I had the technologist paged to call me at home.

The phone seemed to take forever to ring. Finally she was on the line and here is how the conversation went:

Manager: *"Cathy, I just got a call from XYZ Nursing Home. They said they haven't received the results yet. What's going on?"*

Employee: *"Well I did the exam and got it read by six. I was at the office at the fax machine trying to call over the results. There wasn't any answer, so I left.*

Manager: *"What phone number did you use?"*

Employee: *"The one that is posted on the wall behind the fax machine."*

Manager: *"Cathy that is a fax number. Why didn't you call me earlier when you couldn't get through?"*

Employee: *"I don't know."*

I sat at my kitchen table for hours that night pondering the value of communication. If I would have known earlier, I would have been sleeping. Instead, I **lost a 150,000** dollar account.

This show of personal touch will filter out to the customers. These opportunities do not come along every day and one must seize the moment to **COMMUNICATE**.

Customers of all avenues notice when companies stink and have an **OVERALL LACK OF COMMUNICATION.** I define this term as not only communicating information, but also not communicating empathy and understanding.

The communication between employees and leaders is very important, but the communication between leader and client is just as important. Many times customers want to be heard by someone from a higher level. They have a problem or a comment they want to communicate to the top leader. Effective people listen to the customers.

They intake all information, process possible solutions and filter out the unneeded data.

Many times, just listening can solve a customer's problem, but follow-up communications are usually essential in keeping the customer.

Assumption is the mother of all mess-ups in the world. Too many people assume that every customer is happy and rarely uses follow-up tactics such as phone calls, letters, thank you cards, and replacement of bad products. I assumed once in my career and I learned the hard way.

I had a nurse call me with a time delay problem from a nursing home that I serviced for years. I researched the problem, but I needed to talk to the nurse who ordered the x-ray. I called back to the nurse I first spoke to. I told her I narrowed the problem down to two reasons, but I needed to talk with the nurse that night. I didn't hear from them for two weeks and had assumed that the problem was handled effectively until the day I received a cancellation letter in the mail. This letter hit me hard because had I not assumed, I would still have their business. Fate was in my favor, because the company they decided to go with was just purchased by my company. This situation gave me another chance to redeem my failure. I made an appointment with the Director of

Nursing and went to meet her in person. I walked in, shook her hand and asked how she was doing. Before discussing the problems and how they were fixed, I told her:

"Linda, you taught me a valuable lesson. You taught me that when problems arise with a client, you must be visible to handle them and show that you care. Your letter showed me that by me not coming out and listening – I gave the perception of not caring. This lesson will be one that I will never forget. I then proceeded to explain what happened and how it was corrected.

When dealing with any customer problems, phone call communication is not always effective. You must have face-to-face contact to handle the problems. This will provide the customer with the perception that the manager and/or marketer care and are willing to solve the problem.

VERBAL VS. NON-VERBAL COMMUNICATION

Verbal and non-verbal communications drastically change effectiveness depending on the environment. For instance:

FACE to FACE IMPACT:
54% Body language, 38% Tone of Voice, 8% Words

Fact to Face Encounter

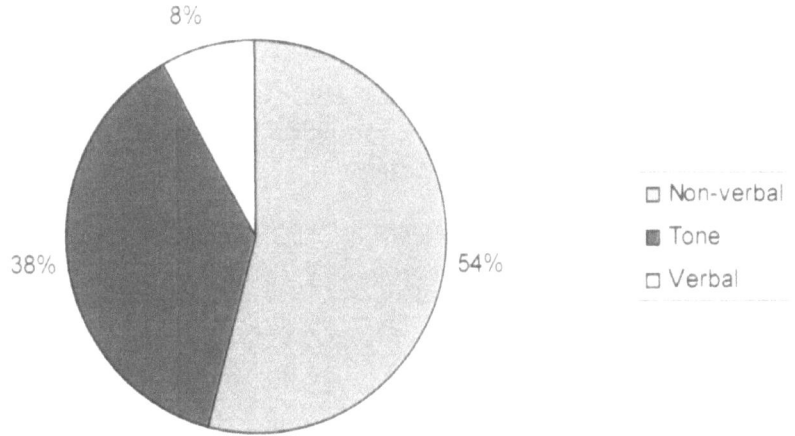

OVER the PHONE IMPACT:
87% Tone of Voice, 13% Words

Over the phone Encounter

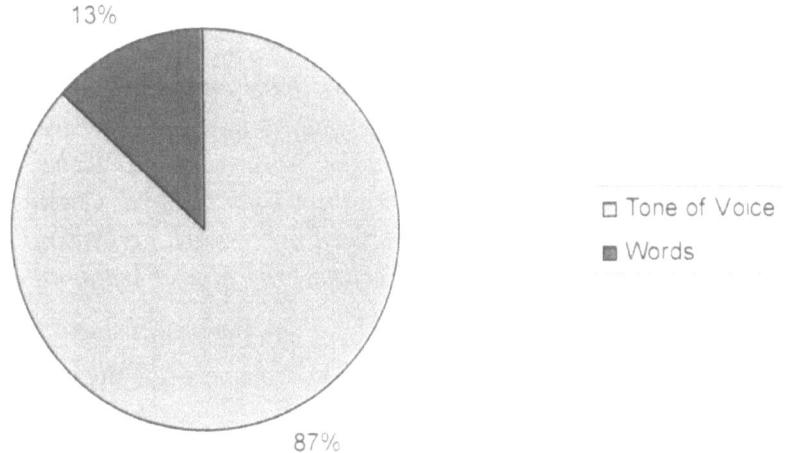

These percentages provide a realistic look at how non-verbal is far more critical than verbal communication. I have discovered that I learn much more from watching people and listening to how they speak instead of what words they are saying. For instance, when interviewing someone for a position, I usually know if I'm going to hire him or her within the first three minutes of the interview from his or her tone of voice and body gestures. I have always had a very good retention of employees and this is due to hiring the right person for the right job.

COOPERATION

Cooperation is the second key to success. An effective leader is able and willing to work in conjunction with employees, upper level management and customers to create:

- *A positive work environment*
- *A productive work environment*
- *A successful bottom line*
- *A team oriented approach*

The leader must be willing to cross the boundaries of employee lines and higher management lines to connect both entities to the customer. Many times the front line managers are the catalysts bringing the whole package together under one roof. If the above entities cannot work together, and then the outcomes are usually poor. For example:

I am a big supporter of the Ohio Health Care Association. My support is not just verbal support, but I have made the conscious effort to help them with donations, being personally involved with committees, sponsoring events and devoting my time and my employee's time to help make them successful. These contributions had to be approved from a higher level in my company and I had to convince them whey we needed to support this association. I became the link between my boss and our clients. The outcome was a definite voice in the political machine of healthcare that significantly helped my company.

Life in itself is in need of cooperation. There are very few single person societies in our present culture or in past cultures. Society, as a whole, has people with definite roles that mix together to make society. These people each have strengths and weaknesses and each person needs the other. That is why each person is uniquely different in how they are and what they perceive. This makes society like a human puzzle; every piece or person fitting into a shape of the cultural pool of success and failures.

A machine operates one major task on the outside, but unknown to the naked eye is the inner workings. The machine is made up of many different parts, each having a separate, distinct role. The belts move the gears, the gears move the crankshaft and the crankshaft moves the extending arm that completes the task at hand. These objects are not alive by any means, but they represent how society or a business must react within themselves internally and with the external environment to complete their success.

CORRELATION

Correlation is the process of integrating personal ideals with business objectives to create successful outcomes. Many corporations develop business plans and generate goals: number of sales, certain percentage cuts in expense and daily operating budgets.

For example, our center provides a detailed MRI scan and report for a patient that has a brain tumor. Our skills and product produced an outcome that completed the cycle of care for the patient.

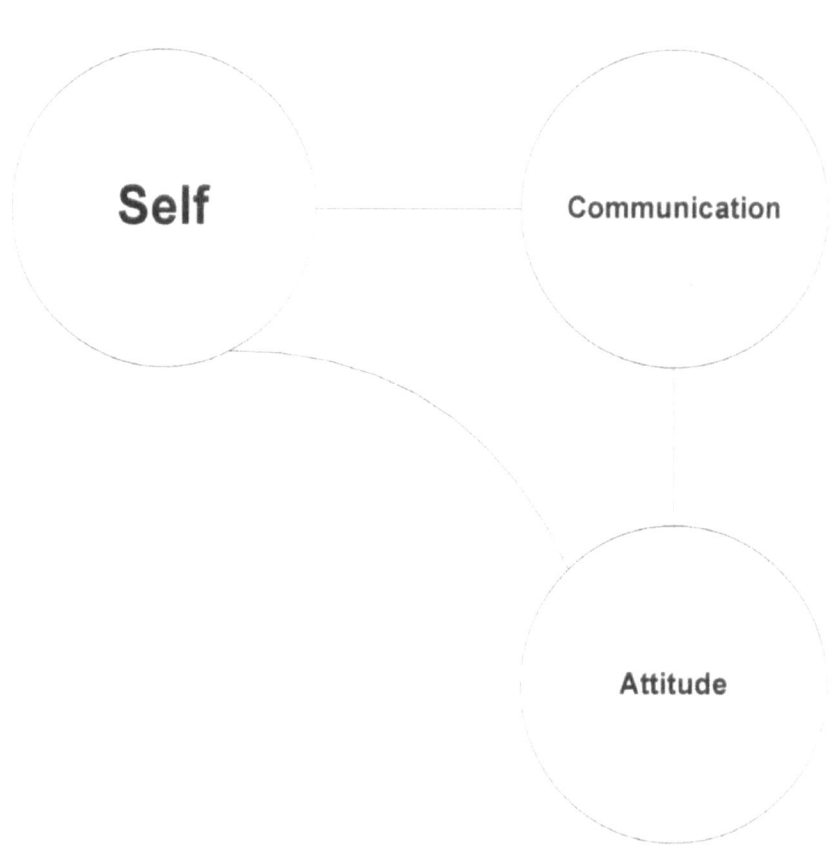

ATTITUDE

"Attitude is a Reflection of Leadership."

Did you ever notice somebody with a real bad attitude? I notice people with negative attitudes everywhere I look. Negative Attitude Syndrome, (NAS) is an ever- challenging foe of leadership. NAS is one of the most damaging causes of failure in business. It breeds in the weakened souls of men and women and spreads like a cancer until the organization is dead.

NAS has some noticeable signs such as:

Gossip orientated communication

- Low customer service
- Low morale
- Negative non-verbal communication
- Destructive behavior

How do you combat a NAS: positively with a positive attitude!

Attitude is critical to the success of a leader. It allows an individual to rise above chaos and positively lead others. A positive attitude can directly affect people and provide guidance in inspiration and motivation.

Motivation and inspiration are two factors that are greatly overlooked as perspectives that directly contribute to the success of a leader. Many corporations feel that it is not the duty of the organization to motivate and inspire its employees to excel within their employment and their lives. One must first understand these two concepts and their true benefits.

MOTIVATION

Motivation is the act of internally and externally creating a positive work atmosphere to produce an employee base that feels good about their work. This concept is usually fundamental within an individual leader to show the employees how to be happy within their given work life. Motivation from external sources can definitely steer employees to excel. There are different types of motivational rewards to use as a motivational basis such as:

- Employee of the month rewards
- Short, hand-written thank you notes of appreciation
- Paid employee lunch breaks for special occasions
- A simple thank you spoken to an employee for a job well done
- Flowers or gifts for an employee appreciation day
- Pizza party in conjunction with a staff meeting
- Tiered pay raise scale

These are just a few motivational rewards I have used in the past. These rewards develop an empathetic view from the leadership level. It gives direct rewards to employees that do well. The tiered pay raise scale can really motivate an employee.

This scale has a top percentage and a bottom percentage, thus creating a very motivated base of employee's interest. If they do well in their job performance, they will get higher raises and if they do poorly, they will miss out. Some companies give a straight percentage to all the employees. The employees that do a good job get the same raise as the ones that don't. This actually worsens morale. Morale is the overall positive awareness of a group of people. Morale can be very harmful if it stoops to what I call, "Morale Deprivation". I define this as the low point of morale that will effect the operations of a unit. The signs of this phenomenon are:

- Employees complaining more than working
- Excessive absences and tardiness
- Poor work performance
- Employees talking about each other and deceiving each other
- The clients are noticing angry employees
- Customer service is at a low level
- Smiles are few and far between all employees

Low morale will create very poor production and decrease the bottom line.

Leaders must constantly fight to keep the morale level high. This is an ongoing battle and sometimes never ending. As a leader, you must think of ways to combat corporate sludge and still motivate your employees. Unfortunately, many leaders fall into low morale and when this happens, it makes it very difficult to get out. When you feel down and sad you cannot implement techniques and/or solutions to resolve or raise morale.

When a leader falls into the sludge, failure will not be far off.

Motivation is not always promoted by positive factors. Many times employees who are having performance problems sometimes need negative reinforcement to motivate them to improve their performance. This technique can be effective if used in the right setting. I think all other alternatives working with the employees need to be followed. If the positive reinforcements do not work, then the leader must go to counseling, create an outcome and one of three things will happen:

- The employee will improve to a successful outcome
- The employee will quit and pursue a new line of employment
- The employee will be terminated for poor work performance

I have discussed motivation from an external environment, but what makes up motivation from inside a person?

Internal motivation comes from a feeling of appreciation. Appreciation is the key for an individual to be productive. The ability to have this feeling is not always present in human beings. Some people are naturally miserable and are not happy unless they are unhappy. They do not have the capability to be internally motivated and are very difficult to motivate externally.

In general, good employees are able to motivate themselves internally by the job they do. I am a strong believer in the thought, "Work for a purpose and not money." If you work for money, in ten years you will be making the same money. If you work for a purpose and work because you love what you do, in ten years you will get the money you desire. Let's take myself for example. I started my career making $9.00/hour. I love my career and developed a great working attitude. Throughout the years, I have excelled to great heights and certainly low lows. It has been eleven years since my first job and I now make a six figure income. There aren't many 28 year olds in this world who make what I make and achieve it by always working for the purpose and not for the cash.

INSPIRATION

Many naïve people would think that inspiration and motivation are one in the same. These two characteristics are similar to a degree, but are vastly different.

Inspiration is the act of feeling an overwhelming urge to relate one's idealistic beliefs and transform them into functional entities in the work place. Inspiration makes individuals truly believe in what they are doing. It provides a base ground level so that they believe in themselves and the causes they fight for. Managers must learn how to inspire their employees both cognitively and emotionally.

COGNITIVE INSPIRATION

Cognitive Inspiration is making individuals believe they have the right intellectual and physical attributes to excel in their jobs. A leader must believe in their abilities and let them create their own paths. For example, an employee comes up to a leader and says, "I just got this task to do and I really feel uncomfortable about accomplishing it."

The leader should then talk to the employee about the task and how to accomplish it.

This will give the employee a vote of confidence and tell them, "I totally have confidence in your abilities to do this".

This will not only inspire the employee to do well, but it keeps the faith in the employee. They have to believe in themselves and what they are doing. If a manager doesn't allow them to achieve work goals and place confidence in them, then they will not be able to achieve **COGNITIVE INSPIRATION**.

Delegation is a key part to inspiring employees. Too many managers try to do too much. When this happens, thousands of tasks usually do not get done in an effective manner. For instance, I once knew a very good manager. He was very effective at what he did. This gave the green light for the company to add duties to his roster. Joe saw this opportunity to shine far above the other managers. He made one fatal mistake in his line of thinking – that one person could handle all the new responsibilities.

He started out trying to do everything and it wasn't long before Joe was not the best manager anymore. I call this the, "**I CAN DO EVERYTHING SWING**". This swing demonstrates the swing from being a great manager to being an average manager due to the lack of delegating techniques.

I also found out about delegation the hard way. I was doing three jobs instead of one and I was killing myself. I had a friend employee who sat me down one day and explained that I was killing myself and that I could not do everything. She explained to me that I needed to take a step back and evaluate myself and what I was doing. I should have people help me. I learned the art of delegation. Delegation provides a leader with the following benefits:

- Provides an opportunity for employees to be cognitively inspired
- Provides an employee growth within themselves and the company
- Educates employees to the true dimension of a job
- Educates an employee to learn how to advance in the company
- Provides a rest period for the manager who uses it wisely

An effective leader also has to accept that employees will make mistakes when delegated certain tasks. The mistakes have to be taken and learned from, and the leader has to use them to educate the employee. If one makes a mistake and cannot learn from that mistake, it makes me think of the baseball player that has a great throwing arm but no fingers to grasp the ball. A leader cannot lose this opportunity to learn also from the employee's mistakes. Cognitive inspiration is also a key factor that the individual needs for advancement in the company. It provides him with the basic tools to advance into front line management positions and produces a quality manager. Advancement is a direct catalyst to this type of inspiration. Too many times corporate entities hold back great employees from promotion because they cannot afford to lose these individuals from the front lines. Employees that are passed by will feel very unwanted by the company, thus stunting cognitive inspiration. I live by the fact that no employee should be held back from promotion. I see that holding back employees is a form of punishment.

Let's go back to our favorite man Jim. Jim has lost the ability to inspire cognitively. He, at one time in his career, had the ability but the V.P. title went directly to his head. He feels as though just his presence will inspire people. People do not get inspired by the *look* of a person, but by the *actions* of the person.

EMOTIONAL INSPIRATION

Emotional inspiration is a less tangible aspect of inspiration. It is something you cannot graph or make a visible presentation on. It is the ability to take a step back and use empathic reasoning to help employees with the emotional strains of the job or emotional problems at home. It can provide you with a certain type of friendship with the employees. Friendship is a very difficult thing to acquire with an employee and if you've read most books about management, it will frown upon achieving a friendship. I do not agree with this. I feel to gain emotional inspiration you need to develop the

"CLOSE LINED FRIENDSHIP" with employees.

The **CLOSED LINED FRIENDSHIP** is one that is defined as a friendship that is true, but has definable lines between work and personal issues. There is a line where the leader is the employee's friend and then there is the line where the leader is the boss.

One very wise man said to me one day, "A good leader can fire their best friend and promote somebody who can pick their nose."

A **CLOSED LINED FRIENDSHIP** provides a sympathetic ear to the plight of the employee. The employee knows that the problems they are experiencing both at work and at home are understood by the leader and that the leader has an emotional tie to the employee. They also understand that the leader has to be a boss sometimes and make decisions they may not like.

Emotional inspiration is most effective when major problems arise. One day my office manager did not show up for work. I called her at home, but could not reach her. I finally heard from her boyfriend, who told me she was in a rehabilitation hospital. As it turned out, she was addicted to crack cocaine. I was very supportive and held her job until she came back. I then sat down with her and listened to her problems and gave input when necessary to show my empathic feelings.

One day, a few weeks later, she came up to me very distraught and upset. She was having a fight with her boyfriend over money that she had taken months ago to buy drugs and she was feeling like either leaving him or getting more drugs. I sat her down and told her I would lend her the $200 to pay him back, but only in a cashier's check made out to him. I then went over to the bank and had the check made, came back and gave it to her. I could see the tears in her eyes, as I handed her the check. I told her "you mean a lot to me as an employee and I don't want you back on drugs and I will be here for you."

Today I have to admit that she was one of the finest success stories I have had the pleasure of working with. She has excelled far above any goals I have ever placed in front of her. She strives every day to be the best she can be. I'm very proud of her and of myself, because of the emotional inspiration I gave and the person she became.

That story is a prime example of how strong emotional inspiration can be. Many leaders feel when they are not at work they can forget about the job and the people who are still working. I have always worn a pager for my employees for their time of need. I could not manage any other way. I remember one night about 1:00 am getting a page from an employee. The employee was really upset with some operational issues and wanted to talk to me. She wanted to stop by on her way home. I told her that she could and I sat up for two hours listening to her problems. I gave her my full attention when she needed it.

Non-effective leaders feel that the workday ends at five and they cannot be disturbed while on vacation. Jim is very similar to this. He does not feel he should be bothered at home, on vacation or on his days off. He is also very difficult to talk to regarding problematic material. This totally turns everybody off from talking to him about anything, thus providing no emotional inspiration.

Inspiration and motivation work together to create an employee that will strive to be the best they can be. One can work without the other, but the effect will not be as big as if both were working together. If a leader does not have both, then a severe problem will occur that I call, **"THE I DON'T CARE THEORY"**. If a leader shows an "I don't care attitude", the employee will not be inspired or motivated, but totally ineffective. In today's age, many managers apply this theory every day. Inspiration and motivation are not easy attributes to grasp, but it starts with two very special words, **"I CARE"**.

Now, with all this said, how is your attitude today?

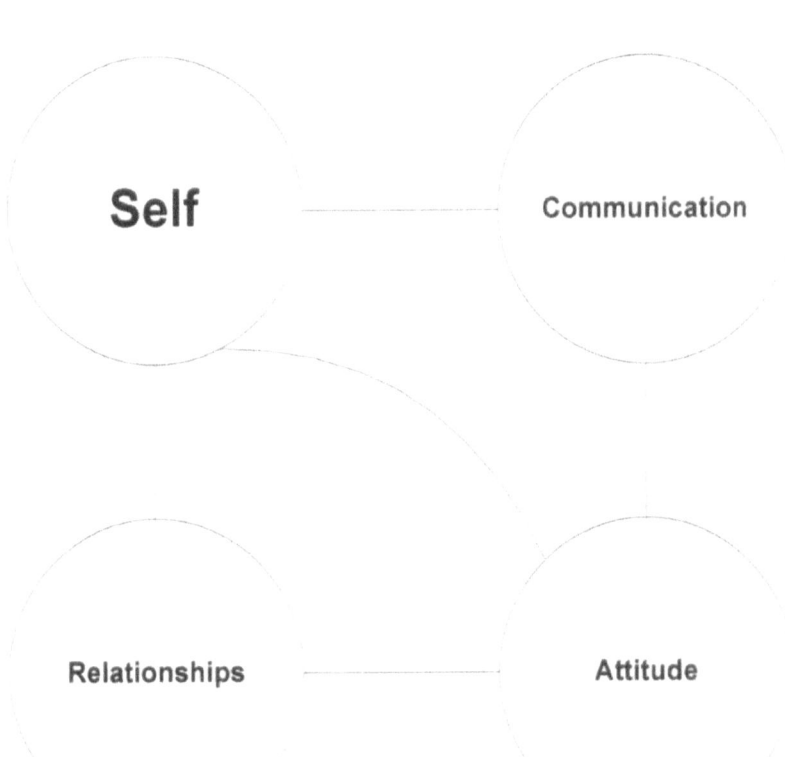

RELATIONSHIPS

"Don't build a relationship for a day, but for a lifetime."

Relationships exist in the world from husband and wives to friends with friends.

In management, relationships are very critical not only internally, but also externally.

The business relationship is a unique mixture of professional mystique and personal savvy. This relationship has to serve employees, customers, upper management and other support individuals. Many times front line leaders have to deal with these relationships all at once, on the same topic plane. For example, I was a front line leader for the mobile x-ray company I now work for. On one hand, I had to make the employees happy about a given subject, on the other hand, I had a radiologists group and yet another the corporation; all having different views on the same subject. I had to balance out the situations with calm, poised, interpersonal skills. The typical business relationship has three distinct parts: **IDENTIFICATION, INTRODUCTION** and **INTERACTION.**

IDENTIFICATION

Identification is the process by which a leader must identify the critical relations in the operation. You must not just look at the internal relationships but the external customer relationships. You must then rate these relationships from most important to least important. For example, here is the list I made for myself one day:

1. All employees
2. Radiologists
3. Top ten customers
4. President Ohio Health Care Association
5. My boss
6. Next 50 customers

You may wonder why I didn't put my top ten customers first. If I didn't have the first two on my list, then all the customers are a moot point. These lists can sometimes change as the day goes on. For example, if I have the biggest client call me with a problem, then it jumped to number one on the list because I wanted to fix the problem immediately and save the relationship.

Identification also allows you to put your entire work environment into a very simple perspective. These are the groups you have to either make happy in what they are doing, or a least make them content. It's like having 10 six year olds and each one wants to play a separate game. To accommodate everyone, sometimes you have to bargain, compromise and be obtuse to get everyone on a satisfaction plane.

INTRODUCTION

The introduction is the most crucial part of the interpersonal relationship. It is true that they say first impressions are everlasting, and they last forever in a business relationship. This first impression can be with a new employee, new leader or a new customer. For instance, I developed a very good relationship with a key person in the long-term care industry in Ohio. He had a previous rocky relationship with another employee of the company who happened to be my counterpart in another region. Well, it seemed that my counterpart was supposed to support this person by donating $75 to an event. The money never showed up, and thus disturbed this person. A few months later both of these people were at a function. My counterpart wanted to be introduced to my friend. When they met, my counterpart immediately stated that he was sending the check and it kept coming back to his office stating he had the wrong address. My friend knew that this was a lie and immediately took a disliking towards my counterpart.

This is a prime example of failing on the introduction. During an introduction, I use the following steps as guidelines:

- Never be pushy or rude
- Never express yourself loudly
- Always make direct eye contact
- Keep all non-verbal gestures to a minimum
- Always smile, never frown
- Always speak softly
- Use active listening

The initial introduction is never for selling or discussing major business concerns. A first impression is the time to show somebody your goals and ideals, listen to them and get an impression of them so you can place them on your relationship list.

If you make a good introduction, this will be the beginning of a new relationship.

Many leaders make a fatal mistake; if they don't get a great response the first time around, then they feel the relationship is done. Upon first introductions, don't expect them to jump up and down immediately.

INTERACTION

The interaction phase begins the true workings of a relationship, externally or internally. This is the part where, over a period of time, you build the upper levels of the relationship. This is where you solidify ties or you liquefy them. These include the follow-up lunches, one-on-one meetings, out at the bar meetings and just plain old- fashioned follow-up. For instance, you just hire an employee and the employee starts. The next step an effective leader would take is; following the orientation period, the leader should sit down with the new employee and discuss common things such as family, job duties, personal feelings about the job overall. This begins the bonding of a relationship.

The interaction can also be very deadly to a relationship. Let's follow what happened to my new friend and my counterpart in another region. My new friend's wife has a consulting practice. My counterpart hired her to perform some in-services, in hopes of getting my new friend's business. When that did not occur, he not only put a stop to utilizing the wife's consulting practice, but also confronted my new friend and argued about not getting his business. This interaction spelled one thing: disaster.

You need to be very honest and true in every interaction. If you go into a situation with false feelings and lies, it will not be long before the truth comes out. I have always found that honesty isn't the best policy; it is the only policy! You must have the common courtesy and guts to speak straightforward and to the point, instead of lying.

One day I sat an employee down who was having a very difficult time. I spoke the honest truth about what was happening and what other employees were saying. This person was very upset and angry at the judgments passed on by fellow employees. I decided to have a meeting of all employees and put a new twist on the situation. I was not going to be the spokesman of the meeting. I wanted everybody to say what they really felt. I would play mediator and let things fly. I was very unsure of this new technique I was developing, which I now call, **BRUTAL HONESTY FORM.**

The new meeting began, as usual, with me talking. I then stated that people were going to speak to each other and address each other. **BAM!** There it went, and it went fast. Every person yelled and screamed. Some cried as anger filled the room. I was stopping people to let others state their own thoughts. Some people stomped off only to return moments later. I was thinking, John this is the worst idea you've ever come up with! All of the sudden, a dramatic change! All the anger and tense feelings had disappeared and the employees started laughing, joking around and apologizing for their own behaviors.

It worked! It let the employees vent their frustrations and to get things off their chests that had been piling up for weeks, even months. I wouldn't suggest the **BRUTAL**

HONESTY FORM for every meeting, but I honestly feel that it can work in the appropriate situation.

Many times leaders think that the relationship with the customer is far more important than with the employees. I do not agree with this line of thinking. The employee relationship is very critical to the overall scheme of things.

An effective leader has to have the ability to sit back and say, "You know I made this decision and I was not looking at the situation from that aspect and I was **WRONG**."

There is nothing wrong with being wrong! Too many ineffective leaders think they are always right and that to admit you are wrong is a sign of weakness. A wise man once told me, "Experience is the product of bad judgment." This short sentence is so true.

There is no way in the world to learn if one does not screw up now and then.

A true leader has found this inner circle of power and understands the extent of its influence. Once you understand it, then you have the ability to know yourself, thus know others and how to lead them. For example, I had an employee once walk off the job. He had some personal problems that, at the time, I was unaware of. I was very angry and thus terminated him without a shred of concern. Two years later, my company purchased a company that this person was working for. My immediate reaction was, "There is no way this person is going to work with me again". This was a gut reaction that I soon thought about in depth. My inner self soon transformed my thinking, and I felt compassion for him. I then looked at the past and decided that maybe I wasn't totally correct in my thinking. I did offer him a job with me and had a long talk with him regarding our past relationship. I showed that my Chi was very unforgiving at one point, but had the capability to transform, mold and care.

Self ———— Communication

External Life ———— Relationships ———— Attitude

EXTERNAL LIFE

"Home is where the heart is."

The external life you call home is directly responsible for your life's happiness.

The external life is defined as an individual's home life. It is the life one calls home.

One cannot realize true success in business without being content and happy in the life called home. There were many times in my own life that I put the firm before my family.

These are times I still regret to this day. It is very important that one balances both work and family life. This balance is called, **The Balance of Life.** This balance is critical to the overall success in one's life. The balance is never in a straight line. There are peaks and low levels throughout one's life. The trick is to enjoy the peaks and master the valleys.

There are many situations that can cause one to lose sight of the Balance of Life:

- Divorce
- Loneliness
- Death

- General family dysfunctional behavior

You've seen a few glimpses of my life, let's take a further look into the early days of my life. I was your typical farm kid growing up in a small town, Homeworth, Ohio.

My father, may he rest in peace, was a 9th grade drop-out and a Veteran of the Korean War.

He was a great father, but did not have an understanding of the new educated world. He worked in your standard machine shop for 36 years and died eight months following his retirement. My mother, on the other hand, was a local farm girl who worked her way into a utility company. She always showed promise, was goal oriented and possessed leadership and management abilities. This combination proved to be an excellent environment to grow up in. My mother would scold me and I would have to explain to my father what she meant.

I was a scrawny, pigeon toed kid growing up in the 1980's. I have one brother who, throughout my childhood, pretty much attacked me both mentally and physically as any other older brother would. This produced a fighting mentality in my already strong-willed personality. I remember spending many days fighting for what I thought was my existence, yet it was really a sight to gain my true call to nature.

I had to then cope with not being close to my mother, but close to my father. My brother, clearly the opposite of me, mentally bonded well with my mother. This actually proved to me that opposites truly attract in life. My family will ultimately deny this actuation just as alcoholics deny their problem, until they realize that their lives have been totally worthless.

Throughout my first 16 years of life, I was always fighting against the odds, without any direction. I was never the biggest football linebacker and never the fastest baseball player, but I was the individual player that put out the most effort on the field. I excelled in sports not because of my physical presence, but because of my leadership and commitment qualities, in their infancy. For example, as a freshman in high school, I started as a linebacker on the freshman football team. I weighed 115 pounds and stood 5'5" tall. At the end of the year, I led the team in tackles in each of the ten games. This wasn't because of my size, but because of my will to fight.

I reached a turning point in my life right before my sixteenth birthday. I started to focus on one sport, wrestling. I was a sophomore in high school when I had my first varsity wrestle-off in practice against a senior. I came out in the winner's circle, proudly to be placed on the varsity squad. This was an extreme accomplishment in this school, because of it's deep history in the sport. I remember that first match as though it happened just yesterday! I was about as nervous and as proud as I could be. My family was in the stands ready to cheer me on. I approached my opponent as the whistle blew and within 50 seconds I was lying on my back with a severe deformity surrounding my right shoulder.

I was carted off to the hospital, where an emergency room physician reduced my severely dislocated shoulder. I spent the rest of the wrestling season in a sling with the doctor's promise that everything was going to be back to normal. As the year progressed, I continued to have dislocation problems with my right shoulder. I eventually had the first of two surgeries to correct this problem. I came back my junior year and produced a 9-0 season until I re-injured my shoulder, then headed back for a second surgery.

I went through the surgery with the intention of coming back bigger and better. I had a dream of winning the state title in my weight class. The summer before my senior year was like a re-enactment of the Rocky box office successes. I rehabilitated my shoulder by lifting weights three times a day for roughly 6-8 hours a day. I transformed my body into muscle. I now had the body to match the motivation. The practice season started as it usually did, except this time I was more dominant over my teammates than I had ever been before. In fact, none of them could even challenge me.

The first match came very quickly. I remember being very nervous in anticipation of this match. I went out to prove my comeback, but it ended in a loss. The second match was a loss; the third, fourth, fifth and sixth, all losses. I then went into the seventh match in a depressed state. Within one minute of the seventh match, I clutched my left shoulder. I left the match and went back to the locker room, where I put my shoulder back in place. When the trainer left, I sighed. I hadn't dislocated my left shoulder; I faked the injury and gave up on my dreams that night. In my mind, I could not live with losing and I could not continue. The days and weeks that followed tried my very existence. Many days I felt enough shame to keep me from getting out of bed. One day I sat in my room, with my parents off at work, and contemplated an unthinkable act, suicide. I sat in a chair with the barrel of the gun pointed under my chin. In this brief moment I realized I was going to die, but a voice inside me said, "John you quit once, will you quit again?" I put the gun away and vowed that no matter what obstacles lie ahead, I would always fight to the bitter end and under no circumstance would I ever give up.

I could not speak of these events for over ten years. These events in my personal life affected me, forever changing my disposition. I let myself down once and I dared not make that mistake again. My personality changed because of this event. I still dream about those events and how they still haunt me today.

Consumption Effect

The Consumption Effect is a situation where a job consumes a person. It's when a person works 24/7 and loses interest in the family life. This effect will directly cause failures in life itself.

Cost vs. Benefit

There is a cost and a benefit to all things in nature. The goal should acquire major benefits at a low cost. There are some costs too high that occur on a daily basis.

"Nothing else matters unless I'm happy in the life I call home."

I think it is important to realize that a leader must demonstrate a need to be at home when at home. It is very easy to bring work related issues at home. I know from experience that is creates problems on many fronts:

- It creates an environment where family members lose

connectivity to the person.

- It allows a person to never shut down from the stresses of work.
- This will actually disconnect emotional connections which are very important to relationships.

I have a very bad habit of working at home when I'm not at work. It was not long before I was tired and ill having chest pains all the time. These chest pains really scared me to understand that I too need down time and I need time with my family not bothered by the worries of work. I improved my day by ending work when it needed to end and taking some good medication to relax.

Character — Self — Communication

External Life — Relationships — Attitude

CHARACTER

"Leadership is teh capacity and will rally men and women to a common purpose and character which inspires confidence."
Bernard Montgomery

How a leader deals with the circumstances of life can tell you many things about his/her character. Crisis does not necessarily make character, but it surely does reveal one's character. Adversity is a crossroad that makes a person choose one of two paths, character or compromise. A true leader will choose character every time. Each time this choice is made, the leader will become stronger, even if that choice brings negative consequences.

Character is more than just talk. Anyone can say that he/she has integrity, but actions speak louder than words. Your character determines who you are. You never separate a leader's character from their actions. If your leader's actions always work against his voiced beliefs, then one must realize the leader may be a ladder in disguise.

Many people have a gift of talent, but character is a choice. We have no control over many items in our lives. We don't get to pick our parents, upbringing and location to start life. We do choose what type of character we want to own. In fact, we create it every time we make choices to stay and fight, or run under the weight of the situation.

Please remember every decision you make today will outline your character tomorrow.

True leadership involves other people. People do not trust a leader who says one thing and does another. People will notice small flaws within the leader's character and will stop following them.

Leaders cannot rise above their own character. I've seen very talented people fall apart after achieving a high level of success. I had a boss who ascended the ranks within the corporation. He sat atop of the company with senior vice president riding behind his name. Jack could not outrun his high exposure to lusting after women. Jack had been married for many years and still chased after women. He fell madly in love with a very good friend of mine who was in a management position within the company. Jack could never keep a secret and soon found himself on the other end of the phone being terminated from his job. Jack called me with words of despair and trouble because his character let him down. Steven Berglas tells of the Success Syndrome, which details the fall of great people due to lack of character. He claims they usually experience one of the four A's: Arrogance, Aloneness, Adventure seeking or Adultery.

I flew the ranks of management very quickly for my age, becoming an afternoon supervisor at the age of 21 and owning my own company at 24. My success continued to grow after we sold our mobile x-ray business. I projected myself to be at the top of the corporate ladder by the age of 27.

I myself have felt aloneness in my experiences as a leader. I felt alone within my own company and felt alone everywhere. This feeling can be very strong and very deceiving. I remember lying in hotel rooms and crying myself to sleep because I felt so

 alone. Too alone to handle all the stress of the job, plus handle the stresses of just plain life. Many people have and do depend on me to make the right decision, every time.

This is a great deal of stress and responsibility for one person to handle. I've counteracted this feeling of loneliness with writing my thoughts and visions.

This allows me to empty my mind, which allows my mind to accept true realities, instead of perceived truths.

Today I have a different outlook on life and on work. I am employed currently to make a difference in the lives of those whom I am involved with. I still carry the burden of the company, people and success, but I finally realized that I don't carry that burden alone, but share it with those around me.

I worked with a gentlemen that had a high level of character. He was honest and forth right in everything he did. I could count on him in every situation to help me make the right decision. He reported to me but I looked up to him. He had all the attributes needed to be an effective leader:

- Courage
- Honesty
- Integrity
- Vision
- Mission
- Compassion
- Empathy

Lack of Character

I had the pleasure of working with many people who lacked character. One particular person comes to mind. Sue was a billing manager for me. She handled the day to day operations of billing for several physician groups. I entrusted her with everything. One day I asked to see the payroll sheet form. I was very concerned with payroll costs.

I sat down and looked through this sheet. My eyes fell upon a name I did not think to see on this list. Sue's husband was on my payroll. He was receiving a fulltime salary for doing Medicare coding. He also worked part-time for a local school system. My emotions went crazy as I looked at this. I was hurt, angry and disappointed in finding this. She had done this without my knowledge.

I realized who she was when I looked at this report. Character Relation occurs when you know for certain someone's Internal Chi. I also blamed myself for not watching the books more closely. I too have to take the responsibility for what happened. Needless to say Sue and I had to part ways soon after this incident.

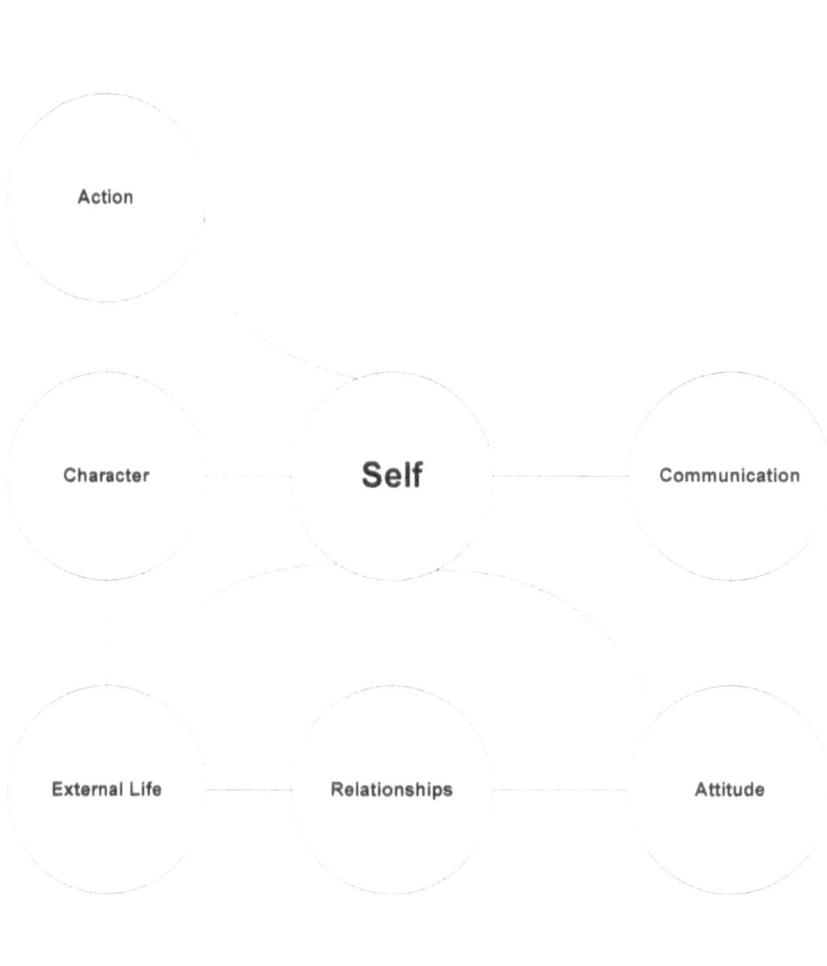

Action

"The only thing worse than taking no action is death."
Vizzuso

Problems and crises happen all around us everyday. Many people watch these situations and turn their head, because they are afraid to move. Problems, by far, are in everyday life along with opportunities. It takes a leader with initiative to take action and solve issues.

I came to a great company who was in need of directed leadership. The company owned and operated radiology imaging centers. Unfortunately, these imaging centers were losing money, had low morale and were fairly dysfunctional. My boss has many talents that were being used in other facets of the company, which left me to deal with my division. I began going to monthly operations meetings that flogged me with disappointing results. I knew if I didn't share what I had learned, this business would be closed within three years.

I concluded that we needed to do three basic things to become successful:

> Increase our volumes: we performed MRI exams on an outpatient basis. We needed to increase the number of scans that each center produced.

We needed to decrease the time it took to get paid. Our billing and collections were out-sourced to third party companies that did a poor job.

We had to manage the process of the business and lead our people.

Now I could close my eyes and walk away from my principles and let the division sink into a black hole of loss, or I could take action and help these people reach the

Promised Land. Many people had tried before me and all had moved on to other aspects of the company. I chose action and then the sparks flew. Our imaging division soon became an imaging center company with over $900,000 of operating income. This transformation took over three years, many hours of hard work and the total dedication of every individual in our company.

THE COMEBACK

I started with one marketing person for six sites. We systematically added four more sites and now have 12 marketing positions. These people hold the task of customer service and sales all rolled into one. In the year 2000, we outperformed our volume projections by 30%.

We had to make some key personnel modifications to spark change. These new managers were more aggressive and daring, which led them to become successful.

The previous managers were either relocated or terminated for cause.

I read a memo from 1992 that stated there was a billing and collection problem in my division. I started with the company in 1997 and the problem was booming. I made the decision to take our billing and collection duties in-house and a new transformation occurred. I promoted a well-rounded person to handle the day-to-day activities of our billing and collections. The results were staggering. In 1999 we collected one million more dollars than in 1998 with a 10% increase in volume.

We now have a company of over 110 employees and we continue to grow. I took the action to make the necessary changes to become successful. It was the joint effort of all employees to make this happen. I just provided the spark to get the train moving.

Problems and Conflicts:

Action Is the Difference Between Life and Death.

It's funny that many people voice taxes and death as the situations that are constant within the universe. I, myself, see another situation that presents itself in all walks of life and that is *conflict*. Conflict is in every form of life from the trees in the field to Corporate America. Conflict is the problematic sensibility between what is right and what is wrong. It provides life forms to choose fate and destiny and decide which direction to take. Conflict is not a simple argument that two entities take sides to try to prove the other wrong. It is a very complex organism in itself, yet it does not live. A conflict starts as a minute form and with time can grow into a health being. Many critics may call this a crazy analogy, but I dare them to disprove it. Conflict has some very distinct parts that make up its complexity:

- Inception
- Adolescence
- Maturity
- Death

I know that you are thinking these are all human traits and thus could not be attributed to a process, which is in all living things. In fact, because it is in all living things, it must have living animal stages.

INCEPTION

As in all life, inception of conflict is the very beginning stage. This is where a very tiny spark of true essence starts. It reflects a true natural battle. In this stage many diverse properties collaborate to produce an initial problem or conflict. There is a distinct difference between a problem and a conflict. Conflict is like a stepparent to a problem.

It feeds it, takes care of it and watches it grow. Conflict has another unique property. It can evolve internally in one's own self or be external to one's environment. Problems are always external to one's self and usually are correctable. Inception, however, is a beginning point for both.

In this stage, after an initial spark, the creation of the conflict begins. In the beginning, there are two factions waging a small but curious testing period. As I have mentioned, these could be two different creatures or just one. For example, a fox is walking in a wooded area and has not eaten for days. He comes across a path and his nose picks up the scent of food. His eyes search the ground and he sees a rabbit lying on its side. At this same moment, his senses detect a danger signal. It is at that moment inception starts. Inside the fox's psyche, two sides split apart; one wanting to attack the prey and eat, and the other wanting to run. The conflict has started and it will run its course.

ADOLESCENCE

Adolescence is the stage where the conflict determines where it will take the entity. This is where problems are birthed and facilitate future outcomes. This usually provides two directions and determines how they will be traveled. This stage also begins problem solving techniques, which I will describe later. Let's take the fox again and see where he is. His mind is still battling between which choice to make and in a split instant he decides to attack the prey. This quick decision has not developed the crucial problem: How should he attack? Should he attack straight forward or go up over the hill and attack from behind. As he thinks, his senses warn him of danger ahead. If he goes over the hill and misses, he would have expended many energies he still needed. If he went straightforward, danger could overtake him. He decides that the hill is the safer and better choice. This stage has not grasped the essence of the conflict and made certain key decisions to not only solve the problem that was created, but it developed the path to be taken and determined the destiny at that given moment.

MATURITY

Maturity represents the actual acting out of the set path and destiny. It is the actual physical and mental battle that goes on in a conflict, such as battles in a war. The given entities have now chosen their fate and move to accomplish the final outcome. In doing so they must show courage, determination, fortitude and persistence to accomplish victory.

The fox now scampers up the side of the hill and then walks slowly to the other side. Every time he takes a step, his danger senses ring out. He moves down the other side and crosses over the path and attacks the already dead rabbit. He has made his target.

DEATH

Death is the stage where the final outcome of a conflict is present. This outcome can be either success or failure. In nature, there are no predetermined outcomes.

This is where the conflict is laid to rest one way or another. In the fox's case, he reaches the rabbit, scoops the rabbit up, and runs off with his catch leaving the hunter's trap still intact in the path, just in front where the dead rabbit lay. The conflict is over and the fox eats his share and gloats in his victory.

Conflict in business is exactly the same. These stages will occur in different intensities, yet they are all present. The only difference is that problem solving can really determine the outcome either way. I cannot tell you how many times I have seen decent leaders with very poor problem solving techniques produce poor results. I had the privilege of working with one such leader. He was a very strong leader, but could not solve problems effectively, thus losing business and eventually his job. This leader would find out about a problem and usually dismiss it as a minor offense. If he did try to solve the problem, he would not include his key people in the process, which totally defeated all his attempts. The number one rule in handling a business related problem externally or internally is:

All problems should be handled quickly and efficiently, no matter how big or small.

Problem solving is a complicated tool that one must master and the only way one could master it is by trying and failing. This technique is not a subject that the local colleges teach in your freshman year. These lessons are learned by on the job training and on the job failing. As in conflict, the individual problem has four distinct parts to it that a leader needs to understand and know:

- Acknowledgement
- Research
- Solution
- Follow-up

Problems display these distinct parts and in these parts a leader must learn how to work through them. Assumption has no place in problem solving and, in fact, many times the actual problem is a systematic symptom of a bigger conflict. If the leader assumes it is the only aspect of the situation, then the actual underlying conflict may not be resolved and take a turn for the worst.

ACKNOWLEDGEMENT

Acknowledgement is the process by which a leader realizes a conflict has developed, and a specific problem is rising to the surface. This process usually starts with the customer calling with a concern or a complaint. It also could be an employee who brings the leader the detailed information. Many leaders make the fatal assumption on the size and importance of the problem. This assumption process is the **BLIND PERCEPTION PRACTICE**. This attitude usually exists within arrogant leaders.

For example, I sat in a meeting one day; the room was full of leaders, marketing people and vice presidents. The conversation soon turned to some problems with the centralized office staff being rude to customers calling in to place their orders. The leader responsible for these employees stated that the true problem was just a misperception on the customer's side. At this point, my inner alarm system started to ring like a runaway fire truck. I then turned to the leader and told him that in the service business, perception is reality and if he didn't change his way of thinking, the next perception he would see is the customer leaving us for a nicer vendor.

RESEARCH

All problems should be treated with the same importance. All problems must play on an even field until the research phase can be accomplished. This phase is a very critical portion to problem solving. A good leader must research every avenue of information that is available to find out the true cause of the problem and not just find the symptoms. All aspects of the environment must be inspected to find the root cause and starting point, which is called, *"Ground Zero." Ground Zero* is the spark that set the field on fire and burned down the forest. This point can either be on the company side, the customer side or a combination of both. It doesn't matter where the blame lies. One must look past the blame and find objective ways to prevent this particular problem from occurring again and produce a solution.

SOLUTION

The solution phase then stares the leader directly in the face. A decision must be made on how to handle the problem and provide the best possible outcome. One must realize the cost and benefits regarding every turn of decision making. The solution must then be effective immediately, either by changing the structure of the given task, disciplinary action towards an employee, or restructuring the external environmental cues.

A leader has to realize that the customer is always right and the first time an employee or leader questions or accuses one of being wrong, then that will be the last time the company has that particular customer.

FOLLOW-UP

The follow-up stage is a very critical ending to problem solving and it still remains the most overlooked part. Many leaders handle all other stages fine, but forget to follow-up and thereby lose the game. If a leader doesn't follow-up correctly, then all previous work was done in vain.

Earlier in this book, I learned a lesson the hard way about handling a complaint. I realized the two critical mistakes I made during the follow-up stage:

- I assumed the problem was small and meaningless
- I did not put may face in the front of my customer to give them the time to share their feelings with me

This situation forced me to develop three different approaches to problem solving. All these approaches include all four stages, but use different approaches and techniques to reach the same conclusions:

- Direct Approach
- Indirect Approach
- Over the Shoulder Approach

DIRECT APPROACH

This approach uses direct lines of communication in all parties of a problem or conflict. It adds all the stages of problem solving to provide a quick end to the problem.

This method is best used when dealing with internal problems. Leaders use the direct approach for internal problems, because they can handle operational problems in a more direct fashion.

The direct approach also provides a stable basis for employees and leaders to handle problems effectively. It provides a menu for respect and understanding from the employees to management. Employees *want* to be communicated to directly regarding a perceived problem; whether the problem is with them or with their work performance.

INDIRECT APPROACH

The Indirect Approach is generally used when dealing with external conflicts and problems. The situation usually demands that the leader move around behind the scenes and maneuver around all parties to go back to the external source with the correct response and solutions. One cannot use this technique in handling internal problems because it can take too long to reach a solution. The delay in time can send a message that the problem is being ignored, which can lead to poor morale and distrust.

OVER THE SHOULDER APPROACH

This approach is the most difficult to manage and the hardest to be successful at.

It is typically used at a management level, higher than a front line leader. It starts when front line leaders, usually inexperienced ones, develop problems and conflicts they cannot solve. Upper management must then come in and view the situation from behind the front line leader's shoulders. Useful tips and suggestions can be given with minimal damage to the front line leader. Problems arise when the management bodies disagree with the methods used to solve the problem. This will create another internal conflict, which becomes a negative outcome. The problem solving processes and approaches, without a doubt, can directly affect a leader's operational success. In fact, it is very similar to handling a medical situation within one's own body. If a tooth starts to hurt and the patient refuses to seek the help of a professional, soon the pain is too great and the tooth must be pulled. If the individual had gone earlier to seek help, the tooth could have been saved. There is a direct correlation between the speed of resolving problems, to the retention of customers:

Timeliness	Percentage of Customer Retention
• No complaint made	5%
• Complaint made, not resolved	12%
• Complaint made and resolved	50%
• Complaint resolved quickly	80%

Client Retention
Customer Retention

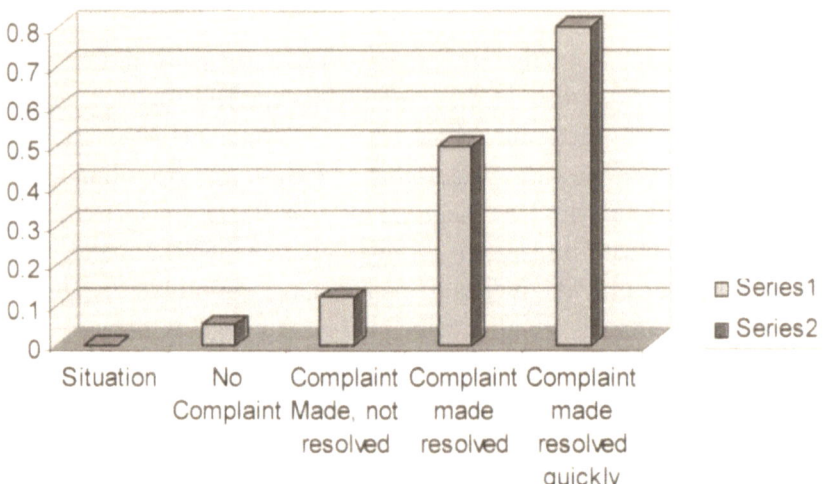

These percentages are averages that I have found in most service-oriented businesses. A leader can solve a problem, but there is a difference when speed is added.

Let's look at the mobile x-ray field once again. There was a particular branch office experiencing a severe problem with turnaround time for their written x-ray reports. They were three weeks behind getting them typed. One day a nursing home called in to get a report because they were being surveyed by the state health department.

The branch searched for hours and could not come up with the report, thus the nursing facility was written up by the state. I was informed of the problem and talked to the current customer service representative. I informed her to visit the customer the next day to explain how we were going to handle and fix the problem. The representative walked into the facility and put out the fire the very next day, which created a good feeling for the customer. It showed the customer we were aware that our response to the problem had hurt their facility.

Leaders forget that problems and conflicts are part of everyday normal operations and to solve these situations one must remain calm, cool and even-tempered. A good leader will not lose control in a very stressful situation. Losing control is not only a sign of inexperience, but a sign of weakness. When a leader loses control, it produces a situation called, "Control Fraud". Control Fraud begins when a leader loses control in front of employees and or customers and truly demonstrates that he doesn't have true control over the operations or over his own emotions.

Problems and conflicts arise in business and in life and, as human beings we must learn to deal with them and provide effective solutions. I guarantee one thing that will happen if problems and conflicts are not solved in business; the management and/or leader will not only lose business, but they will lose the respect and confidence within themselves and the organization. Each time a problem is not resolved, the struggle becomes more difficult and success dims under the darkness.

I now want you to look in the mirror and ask yourself the ever important question:

Did I take action today?

Passion

"It's not the size of the man in the fight, it's the size of the passion in his eyes."
Vizzuso

Experts continually try to find reasons why people are successful. They look at credentials, previous experience, family heritage, personal traits and other items. The problem is that passion in many cases is the catalyst for a person to become successful.

Passion can make the thinned lined difference between success and failure.

Today, effective business leaders have some key elements in common:

- 50% had a C or C- average in college
- 75% of all U.S. presidents were in the bottom half of their class
- More than 50% of multimillionaire entrepreneurs did not graduate College

Passion provides the ordinary person with the spark to overcome obstacles and create successful situations. If you have one element within these pages, please have it be passion, because without it a leader is simply a manager.

John Maxwell, author of *21 Qualities of a Leader* describes four truths about passion:

1. Passion is the first step to achievement.

Your desire determines your destiny. Think of the great leaders, and you will be struck by their passion. Gandhi for human rights, Winston Churchill for freedom, Martin Luther King Jr. for equality and Bill Gates for technology.

Anyone who lives beyond the ordinary life has great desire. It's true in any field: weak desire brings weak results, just as a small fire creates little heat. The stronger your fire, the greater the desire and the greater the potential.

2. Passion increases your will power.

It is said the disappointed young man approached the Greek philosopher Socrates and casually stated, "O great Socrates, I come to you for knowledge." The philosopher took the young man down to the sea, waded in with him, and then dunked him under the water for thirty seconds. When he let the young man up for air, Socrates asked him to repeat what he wanted. "Knowledge, O great one", he sputtered. Socrates put him under water again, only this time a little longer. After repeated dunking and responses Socrates asked, "What do you wan?" The young man finally gasped, "Air, I want air!"

"Good", answered Socrates, "Now when you want knowledge as much as you want air, you shall have it." There is no substitute for passion. It is the fuel for the will.

If you want anything bad enough, you can find the willpower to achieve it. The only way to have that kind of desire is to develop passion.

3. Passion changes you.

If you follow your passion, instead of others perceptions, you can't help but become a more dedicated, productive person, and that increases your ability to impact others. In the end, your passion will have more influence than your personality.

4. Passion makes the impossible, possible.

People are made so that whatever fires their soul causes their impossibilities to vanish. A fire in the heart lifts everything in your life. That's why passionate leaders are so effective. A leader with great passion and few skills always outperforms a leader with great skills and no passion.

I came to Kings Medical Company in October of 1997. I came to the company with a desire to make a difference. I didn't realize that I was taking over a division that in 1997 had lost over $800,000. My division was made up of six medical imaging centers that had many of the loom and gloom characteristics:

- Outdated equipment
- Low employee morale
- Low cash flow
- Tough market place
- Absent marketing functions
- Process deficient

Every month I would attend monthly operational meetings and live through poor results and watch other divisions get praised for their results. These meetings developed an overwhelming passion in me to pull together this group of people and provide a sense of ownership and pride. Every meeting I went to would fuel the fire within me to make a difference for my people.

This sparked a turnaround that even surprised me. The year 2000 actualized a net profit of $900,000 and displayed a team of people I'm proud to say came together under one common umbrella and proved to the most skeptical person that we deserved and earned respect.

Passion is within all leaders. People can tell someone has passion not by the words they speak, but by the look in their eyes. Passion led the employees of the imaging centers to a height no one ever thought possible. This passion created a group of people who own themselves, and what they worked for.

I would like you to take the next day and walk up to someone who you think has passion. Please take a minute and observe this person. Take a minute and look into their eyes. True passion can be viewed in one's eyes. The energy displayed by passion is visible in the intense stare from a true leader's eyes.

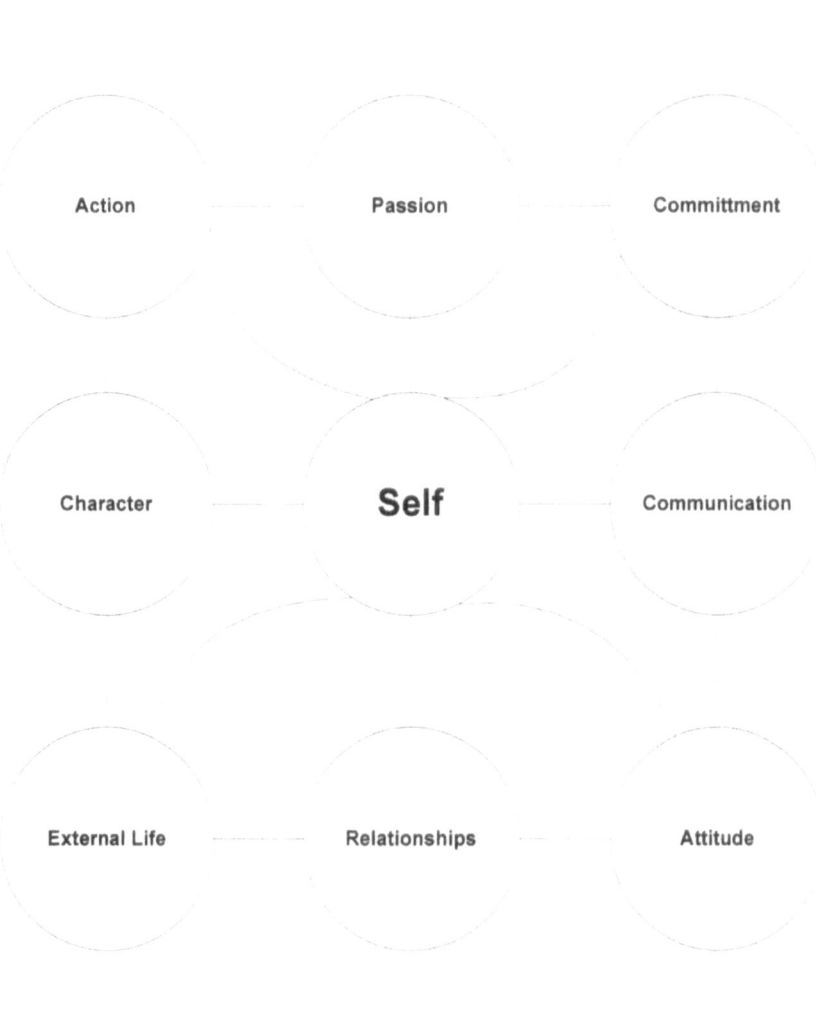

COMMITTMENT

"You either commit to success or to failure, there is no in between."
Unknown

Michelangelo lived an incredible life. He was possibly the greatest artist of Western Civilization and currently the most influential; he was born to sculpt. In his early thirties he was summoned to Rome by Pope Julius II not to sculpt a magnificent papal tomb, but was asked to work on a painting instead.

People believe his rivals pushed for him to get the job because they believed he would refuse the Pope and anger him. He accepted the task with open arms. Once he accepted the task, he was totally committed to the project.

For four horrible years, the artist lay on his back painting the ceiling of the Sistine

Chapel. He did pay the price by damaging his eyesight and wearing himself down. He was only 37 years old, yet he looked like an old man.

Undoubtedly, Michelangelo's talent created the opportunity for greatness, but without his commitment, his influence would have been minimal. The level of commitment could be seen in the fine details, as well as his vision.

I don't think the world has seen a great leader without a high level of commitment. Commitment to me means something to someone:

To the boxer, it means getting up off the mat one more time when you've been knocked down.

To the marathon runner who runs another ten miles, when all his strength is gone.

To the soldier, who goes over the hill, not knowing what's waiting on the other side.

To the father, who sits up all night with a sick child to give comfort

To the leader, it means all that and more, because everyone is depending on you.

I've seen many people over the years come and go, and many of them lack overall commitment. They flow through the motions like a robot. Their motions lack emotion and strength. Many people, through their life, are very committed to their jobs and family. In many cases problems arise that hinder the commitment. **Commitment**

Atrophy is very common. I myself suffered from this in my marriage and in my work.

When Jim came into my life, he caused my commitment to the company to suffer. I cared about the people, but not the cause. It forced me to leave the people behind and find a new cause. Commitment has two distinct parts:

People: We make commitments to people on a business and personal level. These commitments are very strong and long lasting.

Cause: People need a cause to believe in. This cause must motivate and inspire people to commit time, resources and sometimes life for the cause.

History has told us that people follow courage, not titles. Cause and people are the two key factors that support commitment. A person cannot be totally committed without these two factors.

This book is an example of my commitment to you as a leader and to my cause of teaching people the truth about leadership, not what educational facilities want to teach you. I am totally committed to this cause and I live that commitment everyday.

HUMAN RESOURCE MANAGEMENT

"You can measure a leader by the problems he tackles. He always looks for problems his own size." John Maxwell

I remember days in the early stages of my employment career of feeling very afraid of the human resource department. The untold stories rang throughout the rank and file of the employees. Employees would be summoned to human resources and be dismissed soon after. The employees of the human resource department were painted as cold hearted and ruthless people with only one agenda on their mind, **TERMINATION.**

They were employees that were not to be trusted by any stretch of one's imagination.

The halls leading to the department were dark and hollow, with an enormous void of humanity and filled with a sense of sorrow and lack of feeling. These horrors of adolescent insanity filled the inner workings of my immature boyhood. I was 21 years old and running the afternoon shift of an x-ray department at a local county hospital when I had the pleasure of learning that not all rumors are totally false. I was called in one day for a meeting that was being held before the start of my shift. I calmly walked into the meeting room and viewed both my supervisors, along with another man who sat smiling and then rose to shake my hand.

The man was dressed in a well-pressed black suit with a bright colored tie. He seemed, at first glance, to be well educated and equally mannered. My boss sat in his chair and stared at me and then back at this new person now sitting back down. The man had a manila folder in his hands and he began to speak:

"John, I want to thank you for coming in early today so we could sit down and discuss some things the hospital's doing to remain competitive in the market. The hospital has decided to re-organize some of the inner departments of the hospital and Radiology is going to go through some changes. You are the lowest seniority leader in the department. I'm sorry, but the hospital has eliminated your position."

"So you're telling me I'm fired?"

"No you are not fired. This discussion has nothing to do with your job performance. We will be offering a two-week severance package and pay all your unused vacation and sick time. You don't have to finish out the day. You will have the opportunity to purchase your insurance plan. I have a letter for you from. . ."

"No thank you."

I stood up and before I turned around to walk out, visions of my wife, who was seven months pregnant, stared deep into my mind. My eyes went to Ernie, who was my boss, and I saw tears falling down from his eyes. One year before, he threw his cards on the table for an x-ray technologist with one year experience to run his night shift and now he was watching the destruction of a good employee.

That day was one of the worst days of my life. I felt every emotion from anger to sheer terror. This was my first experience with the human resource department and it lived up to its reputation. I hated them for what they had just done to myself and my family.

I now reflect back on the entire situation and realize that it was not a personal attack on me, but a business decision that had to be made to ensure the survival of the organization. The human resource department just has the terrible ordeal of being the bearer of bad news. The human resource department is a critical part of an organization and to be blunt; it is the self-consciousness of the unit and also a necessary evil. It is necessary to play both a role to support employees, and also a role to punish them. A good leader must not only learn the major details of human resource management and the tools within the entity, but understand key concepts in human resource management to provide them guidance at managing employees.

Human resources handles many key aspects to the inner workings of an organization, such as:

- Benefits administration
- Performance appraisal development
- Public relations for internal customers
- Handle internal complaints of harassment issues
- Develop policies and procedures of internal practices
- Maintain employee records
- Recruitment
- Handle internal auditing processes
- Control fraud and abuse
- Handle all disciplinary issues with employees, including up to termination

These functions I just listed are not always fun tasks and it takes all the courage and skill for human resource management people to walk home without taking the baggage with them. So far I have stated some not so good things about this department, but I will state right now, human resource departments are vital to the success of a leader. Leaders need to understand some of the basic concepts that are done on a daily basis inside the human resource department. These practices will definitely make a direct impact between success and failure.

PERFORMANCE APPRAISALS

Performance appraisals are an underused and misused tool by leaders across the bound of gender and race. A performance appraisal is a tool designed to evaluate employees on past work performance. It combines generalized categories to rate employees next to the peers. This is a generalized definition, but there is a complete vagueness left within it. It is all that, yet much more. A performance appraisal provides a stage for direct employee interaction. It can provide a spark of energy, positive or negative. It provides the inner workings of an organization with a support structure for both company and individuals.

Many leaders hate to complete performance appraisals for a variety of reasons, such as:

- It takes too long
- The employees generally don't like to get them
- The categories are too vague
- They have a hard time criticizing a good employee
- Upper management will never let a perfect score happen
- The direct interaction one on one is uncomfortable

These are some of the commonly identified "cop outs" from leaders. These reasons are just futile attempts not to do one's job. In fact, if leaders would just learn the correct way to give an appraisal, they would want to give them. A leader must first set some goals for themselves before attempting an appraisal. These goals will then give a path to follow for success:

> Always be truthful and honest: A leader must always be truthful and honest with an appraisal. Many times leaders fail in one of two ways; either they are afraid to hurt the employee's feelings and lie on the appraisal or they base the appraisal on maybe the last month in the year worked because of some incident.

> Always take the time to deliver the appraisal in person. It is a cry for injustice to do an appraisal without direct interpersonal interaction.

> A leader must take the time and composure to be able to discuss every aspect of the appraisal.

> It is also very important that a leader try to make the appraisal a positive experience for both parties. This can be a very difficult task especially when the employee has performed poorly. A good leader can take a situation that

an employee needs to improve on and speak in a positive tone and encourage the employee to strive and improve on their weak areas.

The leader must develop some achievable goals for the employee.

These goals must challenge the employee, but must not be impossible goals for him to reach. If an appraisal is completed without goal setting, then the leader might as well take the paper and file it in the round file cabinet.

An organization has to decide on which performance appraisal design best suites their business. There are three general styles of performance appraisals that can be used within a universal business setting.

- Open Appraisal
- Closed Appraisal
- Free-style Appraisal

OPEN APPRAISAL

An open appraisal is an appraisal that is geared to have an abundance of the leader's hand written input inserted into the body of the appraisal. In each section of the appraisal there is an area for specific comments by the leader. The sections in the body are all geared to specific job duties followed by an open area to write both positive and negative comments. The conclusion of the appraisal consists of employee goals and a signature section and also includes an employee comment section.

The internal rating system can vary throughout this appraisal. Many systems give the leader several rankings from outstanding to unacceptable. These can be entered or circled, whichever is preferred. This ranking will give a brief overview, followed by handwritten comments from the leader. This is the most effective form for providing an objective point of view and employees performance over the past year.

CLOSED APPRAISAL

A closed appraisal is an appraisal consisting of sectioned portions. These portions are somewhat similar to the open appraisal, except they do not include the open sections for the leader to add any comments. There are very little written comments in general from the leader. In a sense, it closes out any additional comments. The conclusion does put a small area for brief comments and also an area for the employee to add comments.

This appraisal is not as effective as the open style, but can be accomplished in a shorter amount of time. It is generally used when one leader has to supervise many employees.

The leader can still give an objective opinion regarding the employee, but cannot add the personalized touch that can be very powerful. It still encompasses the same type of rankings and gives an effective summary of the employee's past performance.

FREE-STYLE APPRAISAL

The free-style appraisal does not use the traditional section form. It generally is administered in a report, paragraph format. The body is comprised of information, which is typed by the leader. It comments on the employee's general job performance. It does not have any type of ranking system. It also does not provide an area for the employee to add comments of their own. It is basically several paragraphs depicting the employees performance. It is generally used by small businesses that have four or fewer employees.

This appraisal has some real shortcomings. First of all, there are no ranking categories. This category is used to decide how much of a raise the employee should get.

This appraisal produces the opportunity to decide the raise from a subjective point of view, having no data to support it. It also does not provide a menu to follow for every employee. The writer is out in left field developing it as he goes along.

These appraisals can all work, but need to have ties to specific goals for the next year. Goals have to be included with all appraisals. As I stated before, these goals have to be achievable and mean something to the employee. For example, if you try to set a goal that does not directly affect their particular job, then the goal will not motivate the employee.

The goals also have to have an impact on the amount of raise or bonus they will receive at the end of the next year. If there is no incentive for them to reach their goals, then the goals are a moot point.

COMPLETION OF THE APPRAISAL

The actual completion of the appraisal will provide the menu between success and failure in motivating the employees. Successful leaders have learned that they have to complete appraisals in a positive format, even if negative things need to be said. There are many critics out there that feel negative comments are needed when an employee has areas to work on. This is rubbish. A good leader does not need to give negative comments to motivate and inspire employees to try and do better in certain areas of performance.

It is very easy to tell somebody they did a horrible job and they need to make a complete turnaround for the employee to get a good grade. I am not suggesting that the leader ignore a poor performance, because he must be able to evaluate an employee's performance. For example, an employee has done a fair job throughout the year; however, there are some quality issues regarding some of the products produced by the employee. The employee should be commended on the good things done and there should be goals set on the things the employee needs to improve on, but all in all the employee has given all to the job. Many leaders would say little about the good things and concentrate on the bad attributes, which will demoralize the employee, making the goals almost unachievable.

SUBJECTIVE REALISM

In completing appraisals, leaders cannot allow subjective reasoning to cloud the objectivity needed in being fair and honest. One time I had an employee that was a good employee, but I did not care for her on a personal note. One day before her appraisal, she made me very angry about something in reference to her work and her personal life. I knew I would soon have the pleasure of completing her appraisal; I intended to tear her apart from every aspect of her existence.

Well, as luck would have it, because of a busy schedule, I could not give her the appraisal. Two weeks had passed and I calmed down and re-evaluated the appraisal and could not believe how subjective I was. The employee did not deserve that rough appraisal. I tore up the appraisal and started fresh, on an objective basis. The moral of the story is: never let personal feelings interfere with objectivity.

CALL A CAT A CAT

There are never any givens in business and in dealing with employees.

Sometimes certain employees give you little option but to give them poor evaluations, discipline, and/or terminate them. Successful leaders always have difficulty terminating employees, because they truly care about them. In fact, good leaders would rather fire them up instead of terminating them. If an employee does not want to become a productive teammate, then it is like a cancer. From a physician's point of view, a cancer can either be treated by radiation therapy, or it can be cut out.

A leader must learn the fine art of documentation to cut out his bad section of employee worthlessness. Documentation is a key part of guiding your decision. The leader must document every and all situations pertaining to the employee. The documentation will serve as some reasonable cause if the leader has to terminate the employee. All leaders get ready: <u>documentation is not enough!</u> The one draw back with documentation is the fact that it can be viewed as hearsay, and the employee can deny knowledge of it.

The successful leader not only uses documentation, but also uses a discipline policy set up by the human resource department. If the employee is a problem, the leader must use verbal and written warnings on the employee. The documents will detail the current problem, but will also contain the employee's signature to verify their knowledge of the problem. The leader should use suspensions and probation to gain momentum on the employee. Then after all the ducks are in order, the leader should consult with the human resource department. If everything is in order, the employee needs to be terminated.

TERMINATION

I have a saying that I do stick by:

"A good leader should be able to promote somebody who can pick their nose and can fire their best friend." J. Vizzuso

I do not like to fire an employee. I realize that they have responsibilities and families and I do feel for them, but I still have to accomplish the task. If doing something like this does not bother a leader, then I would question their character. I have worked with 400 different employees, and to this date I have only had to terminate three employees and I take pride in that record.

When the leader terminates an employee, it is best to have every incident documented in a letter and waste no time bringing the employee in behind closed doors to confront them. Hide nothing; be honest and straight to the point. In most cases, there will be some harsh words spoken from the employee, but the leader must remain calm, cool and collected and say nothing to offend the employee. It is very difficult to be quoted when you are silent.

The human resource department is a very good resource for management. It can provide not only vital information, but it can be the self-conscious aspect of the company.

They can provide support to horrible situations. I would much rather have the department on my side, instead of walking into another office to be terminated.

Teamwork and Human Resources

Team building, as a philosophy and a science, has been around since the beginning of time. Different cultures, past and present, have used different styles and techniques of team building to provide a strong basis for success. William Wallace, the

14th century hero from Scotland demonstrated not only leadership, but great team building skills. Scotland was in total chaos throughout the 14th century with internal factions fighting with each other and fighting with external countries. The problem consumed the country with each entity having its own politics, goals and rules.

William Wallace, through courage and fortitude, brought a divided nation under one banner of truth and courage and defeated an awesome enemy. Team building is a very powerful tool and source of not only inspiration, but also creativity. Team building produces:

- Completeness
- Motivation
- Inspiration
- Togetherness
- Courage

These attributes can be the direct outcome of positive team building. In the modern age, technology can be a negative influence on team building. The new technology has created a very specialized atmosphere, which promotes individualism in the work place. The technically trained employee creates an invisible field around themselves.

This field creates a problem when someone who is not trained enters it. The trained person takes offense and is not usually able to work with non-trained employees.

I call this problem the **TURF EFFECT.** It is the imaginary circle that surrounds a technical minded employee.

The **TURF EFFECT** can make a definite negative impact on an operation. It not only provides an environment that breeds inefficiencies, but it provides no vision for the organization. It places blinders on the employees to hide the entire scope of the operation and prohibits the organization from achieving its goals. These blinders are called, *"Blind Handcuffs"*. *Blind Handcuffs* are the direct cause why many companies fail, and the reason why most technical minded employees usually do not get promoted within an organization.

The challenge for a successful leader is to take all the different technical and non- technical personnel and provide a staging point where the blinders can be taken off and team building can begin. This process of team building begins with one spark, one individual that will promote enough courage to humble themselves, and also be humble in front of others.

One day early in my career as a leader, I sat frustrated and perplexed on how to help people work together. I attended a seminar on how to deal with difficult people. It opened my eyes to the different types of personalities and why people act the way they do. I realized that all employees have different traits and distinctive views on life and their surrounding environment. Many people don't realize that for them to succeed in their job, they have to rely on other employees. In fact, employees need other employees to fill in their own personal weaknesses. When I looked at myself, I could see the weak areas of my inner self and realized that I needed my co-workers because they were strong in the areas I was weak. This gave me the insight that a good leader cannot make people work together, but a true leader must find a way to show employees that it is natural to need others and it is something they need to do to be successful in their jobs.

This seminar gave a personality test to all whom attended, and I found out many things about myself. I took this test back to my employees and took the time to allow them to take the test. The employees saw their strengths and weaknesses and I also told them how I scored on the test. I took the time out of a busy schedule to sit with them and detail why we needed to work together, thus expressing the importance of working together for the success of the whole unit.

Team building, in itself, is a simple premise based on the willingness of others to put idle differences aside and come together. There are actually three distinct types of team building groups commonly used with service-oriented businesses:

- Internal Work Groups
- Mixed Work Groups
- External Work Groups

INTERNAL WORK GROUPS

Internal work groups are groups that are created and managed from an inter- departmental aspect. The group consists of employees and leaders of a given department.

The members usually represent the same or similar technical background. The meetings are generally used to decide internal operational problems and internal communicative problems. This also provides a place for non-technical personnel to field direct input into the operational issues. This team approach will put focus on giving the employee a chance to have a say in their operations, providing a basis for self growth and help them realize that within them lies the true essence of self gratification.

MIXED WORK GROUPS

A mixed work group consists of all the departments of a given organization. The members represent each department's expertise and skill levels. This group will promote a sense of camaraderie within the whole of the organization. It provides the basis for the departments to understand how and why the other departments work and allows a place where conflicts and problems can be addressed from several different aspects. These groups do have a hard time dealing with smaller issues, like those dealt with in the internal work group. However, this type of group is excellent in developing some extensive quality assurance programs.

Quality assurance programs are a key instrument to evaluate the product or service that is being measured, but also provides a vacuum to look at individual employees' work productivity and quality. Good quality assurance programs will highlight troubled areas within a department. It also helps to have different technical personnel involved to develop hybrid ideas, bringing the best of both worlds together in a crescendo of excellence.

These programs, if done correctly, can turn into one of the most effective marketing tools an organization can develop. They not only cost very little, but they actually show the customer some clear and concise outcomes. These outcomes will directly affect the selling of the product and produce a winning solution for the organization.

EXTERNAL WORK GROUPS

External work groups are comprised of individuals that are external to the departments and even the organization. These groups are commonly named the board of directors. The board usually handles the overseeing of the ethical and budgetary phase of the business. They make the final decisions regarding new developments and the overall direction of the company. These work groups lose all technical knowledge to the other work groups and rationalize where the company is and where it is going.

Team building is also an excellent opportunity for a leader to build those key relationships with employees and other leaders. It allows the individual to see the leader in a different light and provides a starting ground to build a socialistic link between management and humanity. Most employees feel leaders are working from a different plane or agenda.

The work groups help eliminate the perceptions and provide a great start to internal customer relations.

One may say that teamwork groups are a great idea, but the everyday workflow is too great to take people away from their normal duties. The idea of team building is based on the opportunity for workers to get away from their normal routine job duties, to get fresh and exciting ideas on how to better serve the customer. Too many times companies fail to realize this and the entire organization can suffer from what I call, **"OPPORTUNITY LOSS." OPPORTUNITY LOSS** can occur in many applications within a business. An organization has to understand that yes, it is expensive and timely to promote teamwork groups, but what will be the cost if they do not? The opportunity lost is far greater than the original cost to provide the internal service.

What do we really lose when team building is ignored in a business structure? I guarantee that there will be a noticeable difference and it will make a negative impact on any operation. The following is a list of crucial items and ideals lost when team building is ignored.

- Low morale
- Decreased productivity

- Decreased profits
- Low employee self-esteem
- Prohibit delegation
- Enables Blind Handcuffs to control the employee population
- Increases employee turnover
- Produces non-aggressive operations
- Limits communications and ideas
- Limits problem solving techniques

Team building is the component so often missed in the equation of smart, pragmatic business practices. Many times in my own career I felt on the edge of making critical decisions on my own with no communicative input. The majority of decisions made were grossly wrong. I learned that I need as much help and input from all my employees, as I need air to breathe. The team approach has really developed not only my management skills, but my leadership skills as well. Many would say that if you put that type of responsibility into the hands of the employees you are not only foolish, but insane. A leader must be able to put faith in his employees to make things happen. If the leader cannot do this, then he or she either needs to hire the right people for the job or not be in a management role.

I totally depend on my employees to work together and provide a stage for success. There are times when mistakes will be made and failures will rise to the top. A successful leader can realize these failures and grow from them with his employees. As for myself, there have been many times when team building and teamwork ended up with the wrong solutions. Teamwork and team building may have problems if not monitored and controlled. It will, however, give an organization the best chance at success. In today's business environment, lone wolf employees are becoming a dying breed.

They are not only hurting growing organizations, but they are hurting themselves by attacking the root of team building. I had the pleasure of working with a leader that was your typical dinosaur in the modern era of life. Stan had been with the company for many years and had developed his own particular way of doing things within the main structure of the company, which was creating some difficult times for

Stan. He did not want to become part of the team and change things together, as the other leaders did.

Stan would buck every idea and plan developed from the company. He then inverted within himself and tried to be a hermit within a large company. It was soon evident that Stan did not fit into the mold of the company. He finally resigned from the company, but the devastation he left behind was eye opening. I walked into an environment that consisted of:

- Low morale
- Missing equipment
- Unfair policies and procedures
- Lost customers
- Poor operation service
- One of the worst operations I had ever seen

This is a prime example of lack of teamwork in the worst way. The dollar amount of business lost was far more than we had ever expected. In fact, out of a total of 75 customers, we had lost 30. Lone wolves can really hurt a company and leave a mess to clean up. So, I ask, was it worth the company's time and money to provide a better environment for Stan to succeed in, or to pay the cost when it all falls apart?

CUSTOMER SERVICE

"Requirements . . . requirements . . . requirements!"

In life, there are always hidden forces that sway things one way or another. These forces most likely are contributed to just fate in nature. Fate usually goes either positive or negative, which results in an outcome. Many people say it is the strength of faith in a higher power. I will not dispute either of these theories, for I believe in both to a certain degree. However, sometimes the force is actually something one can comprehend by seeing it in action. Customer service is the hidden force within a business. This force will truly decide the degree of success of a leader and organization in the new era of business.

Customer service will employ all things we have discussed in the previous chapters. Customer service is the active participation of all employees to ensure that the customer is totally satisfied with the service or product being sold to the customer. A wise man once said, "A company without customer service isn't really a company, but a thought in the head of a madman."

WHAT IS A CUSTOMER?

To understand what customer service truly is, we have to first learn what a customer is and what the customer wants. A customer is an entity that needs a product or service to satisfy some basic need. There are two types of customers:

- External Customer
- Internal Customer

EXTERNAL CUSTOMER

The external customer is the consumer who is buying the service or product. These customers are very vivid on the price for quality issues. Consumers want the best quality for the cheapest price or the best service for the lowest price. There are some very key principles a leader cannot forget when dealing with external customers:

- The customer is king
- The customer rules
- The customer is always right

External customers are generally needed in all business, because if you don't have external customers, then one doesn't have a business. In fact, a great service or product only becomes great when the customer says it is great and not a minute sooner. The external customer will make or break the company.

INTERNAL CUSTOMER

The internal customer is a customer within the company. In a company, every position has an internal customer. For example, the human resource department has internal customers in all employees. The department handles all complaints and concerns for the employees. The employees are also customers to management in the organization.

The internal customers are as important as the external customers. This statement will be one to live in the memories of all who read this book. This is not a typo – the internal customer is as important as the external one. If the internal customers are not happy, several things will occur:

- The employees will not be happy in their work, which will provide a low morale environment, which will provide poor

operational input.
- There will be a high degree of turnover of employees, which will result in an inefficient operational product.
- The product or service will not hold up to advertised promises and will disappoint the external customer
- The business will lose external customers, making negative changes to the bottom line.

The term customer does not bind both external and internal customers, because each one demands certain needs and desires from the agent deemed to have to produce an outcome for the customer, such as:

Accessibility	Accuracy	Alternatives	Attention
Authenticity	Availability	Caring	Cleanliness
Commitment	Consistency	Convenience	Cost Effectiveness
Courtesy	Discreteness	Effectiveness	Efficiency
Empathy	Experience	Fairness	Knowledge
Listening	Promptness	Personal Touch	Pleasantness
Professionalism	Recognition		

A successful leader will promote all these characteristics and will evoke these in all employees. The leader will openly try and make the external customer perceive that the entire company promotes these values. The organization has to be set up like an open market business structure. Actually in business, there are two types of structures:

- The self-focused company
- The customer focused company

THE SELF-FOCUSED COMPANY

The self-focused company may remind you of a spoiled rich kid getting everything in the world he desires. This type of company pays a lot of attention to budgets and to finding more ways to make money from cost cutting, to increasing the price structure. They usually have no customer satisfaction expectations. This type of company does display some strange characteristics:

- The employees are trained to hit the bottom line and the functions of the job, but they do not know what the true meaning of their job is.
- Employees are geared to please upper management rather than pleasing the customer.
- The leaders do not give thanks for pleasing the customer, but are thankful only when company goals are met.
- All operational decisions are made at the upper levels with no input from the front lines.
-

This is the diagram representing the structure of this type of company:

Front line → First level Leader → Middle management → CEO

This type of company generally outlines what Corporate America is. They do not care about customers or employees. The only thing they truly care about is making that dollar. I have no respect for any company who operates under these ideologies. In most cases they will lose in the long-term arena, because sooner or later the external customer will leave, which will erase the bottom line.

THE CUSTOMER FOCUSED COMPANY

The customer focused company has one main goal in mind: the satisfaction of the customers, both external and internal. This does not mean they don't look at profit and loss, because they do; but they also understand that profit is dependent upon customer satisfaction. They listen to the front lines and customers so they can provide an operation basis to support the customer. They provide good qualities that contribute to the success of all employees, including leaders:

- They reward employees for a joint effort of customer satisfaction and increased profits.
- The employees are oriented on how to effectively use customer service techniques. They know who their customers are and treat them accordingly.

- The entire organization is based on long-term thinking and goals.
- The leaders look for feedback from employees to make good decisions.

This diagram represents the structure of the customer focused company:

$$CEO \rightarrow Leaders \rightarrow Employees$$

This type of company defies large corporate companies. It is usually found in small companies where customer satisfaction is the main tool used against the bigger companies. It represents the underdog ideals and visions, which are critical to an open market and society.

A leader must be able to assimilate the customer's needs while working in the framework of the company, which can be a task within itself. Too many times leaders have good intentions, but get little or no support from the higher executives. The successful leaders find a way to still provide good operations within the company and provide a customer based philosophy. This company is always striving to understand and realize what their customers want. This type of company not only takes care of their employees, but their customers too.

AGGRESSIVE OPERATIONS

Operational personnel are the mainstream of personnel that contribute to the customer service needs of an organization. Problems arise when the operations personnel do not realize this. In most cases, the employees who handle the direct operations do not understand their role in customer service. In the real life of a business, they are the *first* key to success in customer service.

The operations must be aggressive to at least provide a stable basis for good customer service. They need to provide aggressiveness to ensure:

- Prompt service
- Quality service
- Positive environment
- Excellent production

Aggressiveness determines the difference between customer service and customer dis-service. For example, please look at the first scenario: A physician calls into an x-ray department looking for an x-ray report on one of his patients:

Example One

Doctor: *"This is Dr. Smith. . . I need the report on John William, he was in the department yesterday for a chest x-ray. I was promised the report last night, but I didn't get it."*

File Clerk: *Dr. Smith, it has been really busy the last couple of days. I really don't have time right now to find it, but I will get time later and will page you.*

Example Two

Doctor: *"This is Dr. Smith. . . I need the report on John William, he was in the department yesterday for a chest x-ray. I was promised the report last night, but I didn't get it."*

File Clerk: *I'm sorry Dr. Smith. . .if you give me one second, I'll go search it out. I'll have to put you on hold, but just for a second. . .I have it here. There was no active disease. Again, I apologize for the delay. . .I will find out what happened and make sure we fix it." The file clerk then goes to her leader and tells the leader about where the problem is and they come together to fix the problem.*

Example two is a prime example of an aggressive operation. The file clerk is taking the front point in problem solving to help deter the situation from happening again. She also gave the customer the time and respect he deserved, identified and resolved his problem. She then assured him that she would resolve the internal problem.

The problem that faces the leader is trying to make the employees realize why they must be aggressive in their jobs. When employees are not aggressive, they suffer from, **"FEDERAL EMPLOYEE SYNDROME."**

FEDERAL EMPLOYEE SYNDROME is an internal employee disease of non- aggressive behavior that contributes to poor operations and poor customer service.

Let's look at the federal government as the prime diseased organization in the United States. The government agencies are the worst customer service organizations in business. It doesn't take long to realize that the agencies such as the post office really don't care about servicing the clients. These types of organizations promote:

- Poor communication
- Poor service
- Poor customer service
- Poor employee morale
- Little empathy for customers
- Poor decision making

These types of companies represent a disappointment on the economic situation in the real world. There is nothing more frustrating than the feeling you are not wanted as a customer, and not having any other vendor to go to.

The question a leader has to answer is, "How do I ensure an aggressive operation?" This question is one of the best kept secrets in the business world today. We have discussed The Three C's of Success, now there is the, "**TRIPLE I EFFECT**":

- Incorporate
- Intimidate
- Initiate

INCORPORATE

The leader has to create positive and aggressive policies and procedures. These procedures must allow employees to be themselves and to be comfortable in their work environment. One main key that needs to be installed is an employee incentive plan. This plan should be tied to group productivity and give bonuses based on this aspect. The employees need to have a monetary bonus that provides interpersonal growth.

INTIMIDATE

The leader must intimidate his employees in a positive manner. A successful leader will positively challenge all his employees to strive far above their job requirements to breed success for them and the company. Please realize that it must be positive to be successful. A leader may want to use negative tones to scare his employees into performing better.

A successful leader will convince his employees that it is in the best interest of everyone to overcome the challenges that lay before them. It is as though a game was on the line and the coach rallies his players to win in the final minutes. It is the entire struggle between aggressiveness and safety, and aggressiveness must prevail for a leader to succeed.

INITIATE

The leader must initiate a direct role in making the operations click. This aspect goes directly back to leadership. The leader must get into the trenches with his employees to reinforce the coaching. It produces not only aggressiveness, but also respect. The policies and procedures also need to be active and ongoing to provide the operations with a clear and concise path.

CUTOMER SERVICE PERSONNEL

In a company all employees play a certain role in customer service, but the successful company employs a team of individuals whose sole purpose is to provide marketing and customer service to its clients. A customer service representative has to have certain traits that not all employees have:

- Outgoing
- Open minded
- Level headed
- People oriented
- Salesmanship
- Experienced communicator

The above traits create a solid base for a well rounded customer service representative, but sometimes it is natural inner strength that is the key. For instance, I had the distinct pleasure of working with one of the best customer service reps that I had ever seen. I started a mobile x-ray company in November of 1991. When the business started, Portable Imaging Inc., it had only 12 nursing homes on our client list. I met the marketing representative from my competitor and I hired this person from the other company.

Deb was 40 years old when she was hired. She came from a loving family and had over 12 years experience in the business. She had a certain shine about her when she walked into a room, which appealed to all sorts of people. Through the years that followed, I, as a leader and owner, learned many things from my customer service representative. Deb increased my customers from 12 to 50 in one year with the attacking functions of a tiger. She could go into a customer's facility and totally take over a problem without batting an eye, and convince the customer it was going to be fixed.

Deb would bridge the line of customer and friend and that was the key to her success. She would develop relationships with key customers and start a friendship outside of work. This friendship would create a foundation in which Deb would flourish and provide an invaluable relationship. These customers believed in Deb and in the service. If there was a problem, she would be directly in front of them instead of fixing it over the phone.

Deb also brought a key attribute to the game; caring. I've worked with many employees and Deb, without a doubt, cared more about her job and her customers than anybody else. She truly cared for her customer and tried to do anything for them. This caring was evident in her actions and gestures and her customers could see and feel it.

CUSTOMER SERVICE PLAN

Once you have key individuals, a plan must be generated to effectively tackle the market and take care of all the customers. A plan must consist of several aspects of the business:

- Information database
- Development of customer service territories
- Reporting guidelines

INFORMATION DATABASE

A database must be created to detail all the customers and possible customers in the geographic area in which the company operates. The database should include:

- Name and address
- Phone, fax and e-mail address numbers
- Type of client
- Volume of business generated from customer
- Key contacts of the customer
- Any key information about the customer
-

This database can be computerized in different types of software, but I found that handwritten forms work best. A form should be generated for each customer. The form should have all the data information and also areas where visits can be recorded, as in the following example:

Client		Key People	Position
Address			
Address			
Phone			
Fax			
Type of Client			
How many patients/month			
Date	Visit		
Date	Visit		
Date	Visit		
Date	Visit		
Date	Visit		
Date	Visit		

CUSTOMER SERVICE TERRITORIES

Once the database is complete, it is time to create customer service territories. These areas comprise all the customers and non-customers. The areas should be broken down into groups of no more than 10-15 customers, and classified by geographic area in close proximity to each other. An area should be created so that the employees can see the respective customers in at least two days.

A good technique is going to a local office and supply store and purchasing binders with alphabetical dividers. These dividers will serve as the areas. The employee can then carry this binder and record visit information as the employee sees the customer.

REPORTING

It is vital that the customer service representative report the daily activities to the leader and supervisors. A good representative will work a four-day week with one day in the office completing the reporting end to management.

Below is an example of a report form:

Please fax to John Vizzuso 330-656-0600 by Friday each week

Name:_____

Dates:_____ Imaging Center:_____

Date:	Client	Visit
Date:	Client	Visit
Date:	Client	Visit
Date:	Client	Visit
Date:	Client	Visit

These reports should be brief and to the point to give the leader an overview of how the marketing is coming along. It should provide the key elements to ensure the leader understands what is going on in the market place.

MANAGEMENT AND CUSTOMER SERVICE DON'T MIX

This statement is commonly used in many operations today. I had the "pleasure" of working within an organization that felt the two departments could not be involved together! This premise is a sure fire way to fail in business. It is utterly absurd to even think of this situation being productive and useful. This type of mentality is usually bred from operation leaders trying to play power games within the organization.

Trying to separate management from customer service is like separating Siamese Twins that are attached at the head…you get brain failure and death." J. Vizzuso

Management and customer service has to combine and produce a winning conglomeration of experience, fortitude and skill. In fact, the art of management is comprised of customer service components. The following graph details the duties of a leader:

Breakdown of Responsibilities
Leader's Duties

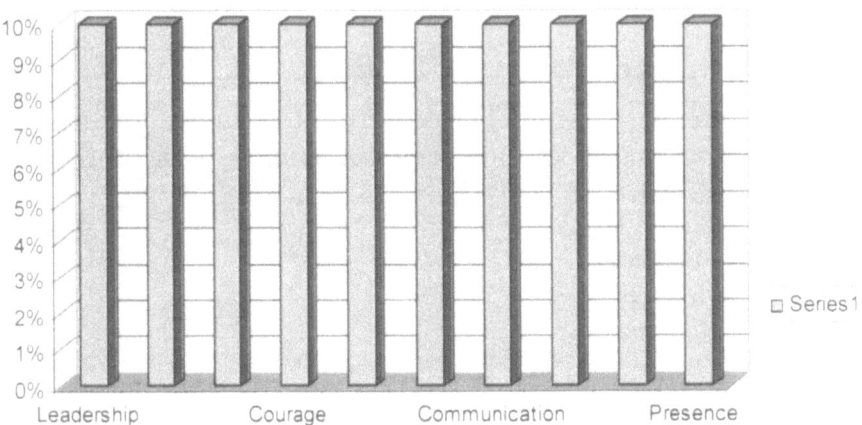

Many high executives would dispute the fact that 30% of a leader's job is customer service. If they do not believe in this, than I would venture to say that 90% of their employees hate their jobs and their bosses.

Communication between customer service personnel and leaders is the most important communication within an organization. It provides a direct link to the customers and market for the leader. The relationship has to be open and up front when confronting problems in the market place. In many cases, these relationships make or break a company and will decide the success of the leader.

CUSTOMER SURVEYS

A customer survey is an excellent tool to use to measure general consensus of customer satisfaction. However, the leader must not replace face-to-face visits with performance surveys. This tool is not there to replace the old, but to add more value to the existing system of customer service. Surveys will provide a variety of positive feedback to the leader, such as:

- Feedback regarding operations
- Details on customer satisfaction
- Reveal unknown problems and problem areas
- Gives an opportunity for the customer to tell the provider what they really want
- Provides a basis for evaluating staff on customer service attributes

WHAT MAKES UP A SURVEY

A survey isn't just some sort of piece of paper sent out to the customer to be used as a scratch pad. It is comprised of three distinct parts that contribute to each other:

- Introduction
- Rating Area
- Closure

INTRODUCTION

The introduction is designed to greet the customer with a brief statement. The statement should explain what is sitting in front of them and why it is important they fill it out. It should also contain a section of the demographic area so the customer doesn't have to fill in that information, but just go directly to the rating section.

RATING AREA

The rating area is where feedback is given. It is comprised of a number of questions pertaining to the service or product the company is selling. The questions should be set up with a rating system that will measure satisfaction. For instance, I am fond of using A, B, C, D, F as my rating characters. It provides a measurement such as a letter grade point average to gauge success or failure.

The questions should be straight to the point and not more than one sentence in length. In addition to the question, there should also be an area where the customer can write comments. This allows communication of problems or suggestions. The area should be big enough so that the customer can write at least one sentence comfortably.

The survey questions should communicate to the leader the many facets of the operation and/or product:

- Response time to problems
- Appearance of employees
- Response time to problem solving
- Professionalism of staff
- Overall response time to service
- Quality of service or product
- Overall service

It is always effective if after the last questions, an additional "yes" or "no" question is added; such as, "Would you use our service or product again?"

CLOSURE

It is very important to include closure to a survey. The closure must thank the customer for all their input and suggestions. It should provide some additional space for further comments in case the customer needs more room to write. It has to have a signature from the leader and a phone number to call if the customer wants to follow-up with the leader. The signature should not be a photocopy, but an original. This will personalize the survey and put a significant value to it.

I have included a survey that was developed by myself and my best customer service representative, Deb. It was designed for Director of Nurses for the Nursing Home customers to evaluate my mobile x-ray service:

MAILING

Mailing may sound like an easy task, but many companies forget one single aspect that will provide the difference between a successful survey and one that bombs. There _must_ be a self-addressed, stamped envelope included for the person to mail back. If there is not, chances are the form is going in the trash can. Typically, a good survey will generate a 40% response. The response will be less than 5% without a self-addressed, stamped envelope.

REALITY CHECK

This chapter has been full of critical information revolving around customer service. This information is a firm reality to why businesses and leaders are successful. Yet, we left out something very important: All leaders should ask the common question – *"Am I good at customer service?"*

The answer to this question will put the leader's world into perspective and create the path to where the leader is headed. I included a self-evaluation test to determine if a person is good at customer service. Please remember the outcomes on a test like this are judged on the honesty of the person taking it. I want the taker to look deep within and truly test the customer service that shows in the everyday work life.

PII
PORTABLE IMAGING INC
QUALITY CONTROL EVALUATION

You are the reason we are in business. We value your comments and would like to hear from you on how we are doing. Your grades and comments to the following questions are very important to us and will help us better serve your facilities.

Facility Name:	McKinley Life Care	Date: 11/26/97
Your Name and Title:	Sue Richard	DON

Please evaluate the following questions by circling our grade:

A (excellent)   B (good)   C (average)   D (disappointing)   F (failed)

1. Response time to call: A   B   C   D   F
   Comments:_____

2. Response time to called report: A   B   C   D   F
   Comments:_____

3. Response time to written report: A   B   C   D   F
   Comments:_____

4. Professionalism/friendliness of office: A   B   C   D   F
   Comments:_____

5. Professionalism/friendliness of technologist: A   B   C   D   F
   Comments:_____

6. Appearance of technologist: A   B   C   D   F
   Comments:_____

7. Interpretation of exams: A   B   C   D   F
   Comments:_____

8. In-service program: A   B   C   D   F
   Comments:_____

9. Response time to problem solving: A   B   C   D   F
   Comments:_____

10. Overall service: A   B   C   D   F
    Comments:_____

Would you use our service again?:   Yes   or   No

Any additional comments:_____
_____

I would like to thank you for your time and consideration making our service better. We have adopted the following attitude in regards to servicing your residents: Where ever you are. What ever it takes.
We are committed to your needs in the current healthcare situation.

CUSTOMER SERVICE SELF-EVALUATION TEST

Use the following numbers to evaluate each question:

> 0 = Rarely
> 1 = Sometimes
> 2 = Often
> 3 = Almost Always
> 4 = Always

_____ When having a conversation with a customer, do I give him or her my complete attention and avoid doing other activities?

_____ Do I make eye contact when speaking with a customer to show that I am paying attention?

_____ When speaking to a customer over the phone, do I make an effort to use inflection in my voice to convey interest and concern?

_____ Do I pick up the phone on the third ring?

_____ When I need to put a customer on hold, do I ask for his or her permission and wait for a response before doing so?

_____ Do I avoid technical jargon and use language that the customer can understand?

_____ When I cannot provide my customer with exactly what he or she wants, do I suggest options and alternatives?

_____ Do I sincerely apologize to the customer when a mistake has been made by my company or me?

_____ When a customer is voicing a complaint, do I remain calm and understandingeven if I think he or she is wrong?

_____ Do I view customer service complaints as an opportunity to improve service rather than as a problem that is taking up valuable time?

_____ Do I treat my employees as customers?

_____ TOTAL SCORE

RESULTS

0-12 Points, You're at the Bronze Level
13-22 Points, You're at the Silver Level
23-30 Points, You're at the Golden Level

BRONZE LEVEL

This doesn't mean you don't care about your customers. This either means you're new to the service field or you are a seasoned veteran that is rusty on customer service.

SILVER LEVEL

You have a solid understanding of the basics, but you are not using them consistently probably due to being overwhelmed by your job functions.

GOLD LEVEL

Congratulations! You are a professional at providing service.

HONESTY THE ONLY POLICY

One day I was in the middle of some very poor operational services.

These services produced some very bad situations for our clients. I walked into an

office where the assistant leader was waiting for me with the details of a problem.

We were going over to the client's office to explain what happened. He walked up to me and said:

"John, I've got this figured out. We'll tell him that they had the information we needed to process the x-ray and because we didn't have it, then it couldn't be processed. This will throw the blame on them relieving us." "Did we need the information", I asked.

"No, we should still have had it done, but this will get us off the hook."

"Ed, if you want to go and lie to these people, then go by yourself. I am not going to lie."

When problems arise, it is best to tell the truth. It is unethical to make up excuses that are false. The customer will figure out the lie and you will lose that customer for life. If you are honest and lose the customer then maybe sometime in the future, you'll be able to get that customer back. If you lie, then you are only hiding your own guilt and dishonesty.

The end of this chapter should be a true-life situation that adheres to the principles of customer service and should win The Vizzuso Award for Customer Service. One day I sat in a local fast food establishment in Hudson, Ohio. I was on my lunch break and sat down to enjoy a paper and some fattening food. I was lost in the news events of the day when I heard harsh words coming from my left. My eyes and attention were now focused on the booth across from me.

A man was sitting there with a disturbed look on his face. He then proceeded to yell at one of the employees who had come over to see what his problem was. He yelled, he cussed, until this poor girl ran back crying to the restaurant manager. The manager took over and approached the man with a very pleasant smile on his face. The man then started yelling at the restaurant manager. He claimed to have given the girl a ten dollar bill, but received change for a five dollar bill. He demanded his correct change.

The manager looked at this irate customer and could understand his concern. The irate customer suggested that either the girl was stealing his money or she was poorly trained. The very controlled manager spoke softly and expressed his assurance that the employee was a good employee, with over eight years experience. This enraged the customer even more, who was now standing and yelling that he didn't care about what the employee was like, he wanted his correct change.

The manager did say that he would be glad to give his money back, but his protocol dictated that he would have to cash out the drawer and provide documentation that the event occurred. This made the customer really mad because he felt that he was being called a liar. At that moment, the restaurant manager said he would take care of the situation and went back to the counter. He returned to the customer with the seven dollars and said, "Sir, here is your seven dollars, since you are pressed for time, I took it out of my own pocket. I apologize for any problems this may have caused you and I hope you have a great day." His words came out with that same pleasant smile on his face.

I gave this man *"The Vizzuso Award for Customer Service"*, because he not only handled a customer with respect and honesty, but defended his employees' ethics and intentions. He provided the customer with what he wanted and provided his employee with the assurance that she did nothing wrong. In customer service, leaders have to be complete in their actions, or the outcomes will provide incomplete success.

Corporate Culture

"You're in or you're out"

Corporate America, the surge of the business world is nothing more than vanity gone wild. In the beginning of this book, I detailed what Corporate America thinks a good manager is. It truly loves the managers with many of the negative attributes that I have previously detailed. It provides encouragement for managers to be uncaring, unethical, single-minded, goal oriented creatures. Many times I have wondered why would the beast want its warriors to be like that. It comes down to control. The beast wants to have druids in business suits to do its bidding in the business world.

The beast hates free thinking employees. The free thinker is a threat to its power and control. A free thinker may realize the hidden agendas, illegal ventures and flawed systems. The thinker may jeopardize the hierarchy of overpaid, do nothing chief operating officers. The thinker may realize the company's weaknesses and decide to compete in the same market and bring a new, fresh competitor to do battle on the battlefield of paper and vision.

The free thinker may attach themselves to other employees, who would otherwise be wheels of the machine. The thinker may make them start to think for themselves and thus start an expansion of free, vision-oriented thinking. Then the masses gather and defy the scientific modeled managers and resist the strength of the beast.

However, in the beast all across America, are many free thinkers trapped by its power. How do these inspirational people survive the day to day pressures of the job?

It's a terrible injustice in life for these people to have to suffer day in and day out. If you are one of those free thinkers, there is hope and sunshine, because I am positive proof that you can survive and you can grow within yourself and defy the odds. Please understand the road is hard and long and it will take every ounce of energy to make it. It's ironic that in the midst of finishing this book, I came to grips with my employer. I had to make some tough decisions. It started back in 1993 when my partners and I sold Portable Imaging, Inc., to Symphony Mobilex.

Symphony was the largest mobile x-ray company in the United States. A larger company owned them, which is a publicly held company called Integrated Health Services. This was my first shot at working for a large corporation. I stayed on and managed my location and enjoyed the operations, because I was responsible for my own business, as I had been in the past.

I noticed that the other managers who had been acquired along with my company were not adjusting to the new corporate structure. It would not allow them to do things as they had done in the past and moved slowly at handling key issues. These managers were good at what they did, but had different opinions than the company. I watched as one by one they fell to termination over the next couple of years. I, myself, sat back and watched as they fell from the ranks and I soon received a promotion to Director of Operations for the entire region.

This promotion was something that inspired me to prove my worth to the company. I reflect back on the entire situation and now realize that the promotion itself was a hollow victory. I believed in what the corporation wanted and stopped at nothing to make sure the goals were met, and if the other manager's didn't fit in, then I would assist in removing them. I started to climb that corporate ladder of gold by stepping on those around me. These are times that make me ill to think of what happened and ashamed of my own actions, which were blinded by the corporate beast. I make no excuses for my actions, only regret them with all my heart and soul.

The director of operations was a learning experience for my own good. I started to see what the true nature of the beast was out to get . . . the bottom dollar and at any expense.

My boss was a good man who struggled every day to do the right thing. Unfortunately, he strayed from the path one too many times and also was terminated. I was then asked to take over his job and continue in my current position, as well. The COO assured me that I would receive all the support necessary to continue the business in the right direction.

The months rolled by with no formal title change; just fill-in "gofer". I was entitled to a raise in October of 1996 and was told that I would have to wait until January of 1997 for my raise. This gave me the impression that with the start of a new budget, I would be promoted to the Vice President job! Two weeks after telling me about my raise, I was informed that they had promoted another person to the position from a different region.

That was one of the most disappointing days in my business life. The corporation basically used me to be a stop gaps measure until they wanted to go somewhere else. I was told I did a good job, but they wanted this new person to come in and take the position. It bothered me knowing that my services were being taken for granted and prompted me to think about the ethical boundaries of the company.

The new vice president came in and you guessed it, his name was Bob. If you remember, Jim was the example that I used earlier in the book. He came in from a different region and spoke many encouraging words. In the midst of this change, our Marketing Director stepped down and I was expected to fill in the void. I was now doing two jobs for the price of one, and I began to open my eyes into the heart of the beast.

The following months served as an eye opening experience for my business life. Jim was exactly the opposite from what he said he would be. He was a power hungry dredge of society. He felt that all the employees in the region were inferior to him and his position and he spoke down to everyone. I began to see what the corporation wanted in a manager and I could not, and did not want to be that type of person.

The months went by, and day-by-day, I saw myself not wanting to be involved with the company. There had been some unethical activity within the company, which started to wear on my conscience. I didn't agree with some of the new practices of hiding the truth from our customers.

Then the new policies and procedures started to change. Individuals developed the new changes with no practical operational experience in the business. They were not only foolish, but hurt the front line employees of the company. For instance, the x-ray technologists were paid a monthly bonus based on the number of patients they did. The company was taking away the incentive program that these employees used to pay their house and care notes. This was such a disastrous move that it brought chills to my body. I was a manager in a company and had to lie and smile to try and convince them that everything was going to be ok. Employees are not that easily fooled and they all could see the truth of the situation.

The terrible decisions continued to occur, which now affected the operations. The service, which had been good for so long, was beginning to fall apart. Bob was too arrogant to realize what was happening. I would attend meetings and try to make him aware of the growing problems in the field, and he would totally ignore me. The changes kept surfacing, each one made with a more illogical reason. To be honest, I had the best diet selling in the healthcare market, called Stress Salad. The individual doesn't eat, doesn't sleep and worries all the time. This diet helped me lose 20 pounds. The only problem is you won't survive if you stay on it too long!

The days turned into long miserable episodes of going to customers and trying to ask for forgiveness in a world of mud. I could now see that the corporate life I deemed to be part of myself drifting into the night and starting to feel like an outcast. This corporate outcast example is one many employees at some time in their career feel, but can't put a name to it. It's when the employee does not feel the same as the company and soon starts to disassociate from the main focus of the company. In fact, most of the managers who had been fired previously, had this outcast mentality. I could not continue in the path set before me and this presented a horrible situation. I had two paths to chose:

Look for other employment opportunities

• Resign immediately

I didn't have that third option of conforming and becoming part of the new clique, and I knew it. Successful managers that promote good leadership skills cannot become silent partners and watch as the company fails. They cannot sit back and watch everything they had built be destroyed overnight and most of all, they cannot see employees who had followed them treated in such a poor manner. I knew, without a doubt, that if I didn't change jobs, I would be terminated within six months.

Corporations hold a very strong bond over all the employees called **EQUITABLE WORTHLESSNESS.** This is when they verbally relay message of salaries to the employees. They will verbally explain that their employees and managers will never find a job in the marketplace making the same money or more money than they already do. This is a very powerful illusion they try to spread throughout the organization. They also use the, "Time In" scenario. This is where they feel they can treat the employee badly because they know the person will not leave the company after having been employed by them for so many years.

I started sending out resumes and cover letters into the night hoping that it would bring me the wish I so desired to receive. I walked into the house one day, my wife standing in front of me, asking if I still liked my job. She had noticed that I had been very unhappy. I had to be honest and tell her the entire story of what was taking place. I went out to mow my grass, and out of the blue I was called to the phone, it was an employment recruiter. I sent my resume to this recruiter four years prior and he called unexpectedly with a job he thought would interest me.

The new position was with a local company called King's Medical Company, as an operations manager, supervising six medical imaging centers across the United States. The asking salary was a littler lower than mine, but the company had a better bonus program, so I agreed to a phone interview with a man named Carl.

The morning of the phone interview was a nervous time for me, because I hadn't interviewed in over ten years. The appointed time came and went – Carl didn't page me. In my anxiety, I called him and left a message. Gratefully, he soon called me back and we talked for an hour or so. I could feel that I had some of the key qualities they were looking for, and Carl and I had a lot of the same ideas. We scheduled a face-to-face interview the following Monday.

I traveled to King's Medical Company on Monday and felt very apprehensive, as there was more riding on this interview. I had my total career as a manager on the line. All my ideals and vows that were being shattered by Symphony Mobilex wanted to be heard by an objective ear and I not only wanted, but needed a new start.

I walked into the building where all my life's work was on the line and went into the interview confident in my own abilities and what I stood for. I met Carl Kozlowski. He was a rather average looking man, but there was something in his eyes that reminded me of something – I just couldn't place the memory. We talked for a while, he asked specific questions about what I would do if I got the position. I left the interview and in an instant, I remembered what that look was. I saw that same look in the mirror every morning; it was the look of a born leader. Carl surely could sense the same look within me and the two of us bonded somewhat at the interview.

I was called back for five more interviews with other key employees of the company. These other managers were from different divisions, but all had the same ideals and convictions. The days that followed the interview were indeed difficult to handle. I had so many hopes and dreams riding on this one cliff and I could so easily miss the edge and fall off. Then I received a call from Carl one morning offering me the position with a salary higher than I was currently making. I was traveling to Columbus, Ohio to attend a meeting that day. I rolled down my window and let out a yell heard by all.

I went into the corporate office at my current job and immediately typed a resignation letter. As I typed, reflections on the past kept running through my mind. I enjoyed being respected by many of my peers and didn't want to leave them. The feeling of staying was almost too powerful for me, but I knew in my heart that I had to move on. I no longer believed in Symphony Mobilex and the upper management levels. To me, if you don't believe, then it's time to find another cause to fight for.

I walked up to Jim and handed him my letter, standing my ground with pride and determination. I smiled as I spoke of the reasons for my leaving and left his office without a handshake. I did it! I told a $150 million dollar company that it couldn't defeat me nor beat my will. I showed them that a motivated, confident person could take his inner abilities, add something to them and provide a new basis for personal growth. As I walked out, Jim made one comment that really revealed his insecurity and stupidity. He said, "Well, we'll probably buy your new company some day anyway". This comment told me that he was as full of bull as I thought. I walked out the door and would start my new life in 30 days. The countdown began. The news went through the ranks like a wild fire.

The 30 days dragged along and I felt uneasy as I performed the functions of my job. During that time, I said my good-byes to many of my customers that had believed in what I did for all those years. The last day arrived and I said my final words to the employees who meant the most to me. I drove away the last day and tears rolled down my cheeks, not only for the sadness I felt leaving the people who became a second family to me, but I was scared to death about starting my new job.

I walked into the new office with a smile on my face and a strange new feeling overcame me as I met the other employees and the day went on. All the employees smiled as they performed their job duties. The positive attitude filled the entire building.

I walked into my office, which they had just remodeled for me, and I was shocked. The office was done perfectly and I was amazed that I didn't have to ask for anything. This was the first day that I got to know Carl a little better. He is me – ten years from now. I can see myself learning a lot from him and what he represents. This smaller company definitely is far more compassionate to its employees. I found the following qualities that I genuinely missed by being part of a large corporation:

- Open communication
- Positive attitude
- Employee satisfaction
- Leadership from higher management
- Fresh atmosphere
- Proactive problem solving
- Education and training for employees

I had six sites across the United States I was responsible for and was taking the job with the wisdom learned from the beast itself. I am very cautious about making any giant changes within the operational structure. Jim showed me what this would do to morale, as he destroyed it within six months. I have encouraged all the employees on all the points that I have stated in this book. I am growing within myself, as I grow with all my employees, to succeed in our business line.

Many will ask, why did John write about this experience? I want to yell as loud as I can across the United States, that you can survive and beat the beast! It is not an impossible task. It isn't impossible for the old timers either.

I had to leave behind a manager and a friend by the name of Jeff. Jeff had been working with the company for over 15 years. He actually took my place in the company without a promotion and lost money in his salary. Jeff seems to be miserable in his job and with the company. Jeff, being in his mid forties, feels he doesn't have a choice but to stay with the beast. Jeff has to then conform his actions to the way of the beast.

This action of giving in is called, **SUBMISSION CONFORMITY.** **SUBMISSION CONFORMITY** is when an employee gives up and conforms to ideals and ethics that are part of the beast and not of the employee, himself.

Many people would say if Jeff doesn't like his job then why wouldn't he go out and find another one? The process for employees like Jeff is not clear cut, but clouded by many things such as:

- The employee usually lacks confidence in his own ability. This lack of confidence is most likely clouded within themselves and is not a true perceptive reality.
- The employee fears change within their environment and within their own inner-self.
- The employee doesn't want to lose time served with the current company
- In the end, the employee does not want to lose everything he has worked for.
-

The last bullet point is the most frustrating for me to understand. In my eyes, they have lost all that is true when they conform to the ideals they don't believe in. Jeff has lost himself and his ideals. To me he is lost in the business world and has become a slave to the beast. I remember Jeff telling me that he had too much to risk if he left. My response to him was, "Do I risk less?"

WHAT DOES IT TAKE TO BEAT THE BEAST?

The question every good employee and manager should want to know is this:

How do you beat the corporate beast? There is one major thing the person has to do and that is *totally believe in one's own ability*. You must have confidence to go into any situation and know that your abilities will provide you with the opportunity to be successful. There is a term for this, **CONSCIENCE CONFIDENCE**, which is the confidence a person projects to all the people around his business environment. **UNCONSCIENCE CONFIDENCE** is the most important factor to have. This is confidence that is within a person that is used to help him strive far above the rest.

There are other actions that will help an individual survive the beast long enough to find an employment opportunity:

- The person has to remain silent about their intentions in leaving the company. If the knowledge gets to the wrong people then he/she may be a target of the higher management side.
- The employee needs to document their troubles, and have a paper trail in case the manager may want to discipline.
- The employee or manager must not go to their manager's supervisor with the problems that are occurring. This will ensure termination in a short time.
- The employee cannot trust any employee, even his closest friend
- The person must actively pursue a new job.
-

Lastly, you cannot give up or give in to the beast. The employee that keeps their free thinking and ideals, is an employee that someday will turn into a manager, probably not with the beast, but with a smaller company. Everyday in the business world employees sell themselves out and other employees for fame and fortune. They believe the best way up the corporate ladder is by stepping on the heads of weaker employees and managers.

The true employee will work for the job at hand and the vows and ideals that are embedded in them. The manager or employee should work for the cause and not the money. If a person works for money only, then ten years down the road, they will still be working for that same dollar. If the person works for the cause and works hard, then the money will come to them. It is a misfortune in this world that so many people have to hurt others to be promoted.

The beast is very powerful and awesome. It can determine the success rate of countries and other business lines. It cannot be caring and it does not care about the individuals that makes it successful. It looks at the individual that tries to make a difference and think for them, and laughs. It seems as though there is nothing out there that can hurt it or defy it. It provides growth for a select few and denies all others access. It has enough money to outlast depressions and enough sense to be ruthless in business. It feels like everything out there will be crushed by its power. Many people and events in history remind me of the beast.

The English government thought they had a strong hold on America, yet a defiant young America sacrificed many things to bring the great nation to its knees and birth a brand new start.

All in all, the beast can be defeated. It can be approached and changed if an individual has enough courage to do it. It can be done and anyone can do it. I have traveled the road and have realized my own faults and my own successes, but I have survived the jaws of the beast and excelled from it. I live as all men live, and I will never let the beast out of my sight wherever I go.

QUOTES TO LIVE BY

"Words and swords are alike; they both can be double edged." J. Vizzuso

Throughout this book I have included some quotes that I have always believed in. I enjoy reading different quotes and have developed some quotes of my own. This chapter will detail all the quotes from myself and some from other people in history. These quotes are words to take in and realize what they truly mean. Words can mean the world or mean nothing depending on how they are perceived.

QUOTES TO LIVE BY

"There is no change, no destiny, no fate, that can circumvent or hinder or control the firm resolve of a determined soul."

- Ella Wheeler Wilcox

"Give, and it will be given to you; good measure, pressed down, shaken together, running over, they pour into your lap. For by your standard of measure it will be measured to you in return."

- Luke 6:38

"Problems are big when problem solving techniques are small."

153

John Vizzuso

"The way you treat your employees is the way you treat your customers."

- Tom Reilly

"Fail to honor people, they fail to honor you; but of a good leader, who talks little, when his work is done, his am fulfilled, they will all say, we did this ourselves."

- Lao Tzu

"I have a dream."

- Martin Luther King, Jr.

"Heroes are always remembered and legends never die."

- Babe Ruth

"If you dream it. . .you can do it."

- Walt Disney

"All men dream, but not equally. Those who dream by night in the dusty recesses of their mind awake to find that it was in vanity; but the dreamers of the day are dangerous men, that they may act their dreams with open eyes to make it possible."

- T.E. Wilson

"These are the hard times in which a genius would wish to live. Great necessities call forth great leaders."

- Thomas Jefferson

"Don't get defensive. . .get busy."

- Tom Reilly

"A manager without leadership is like a car without gasoline. . .it just won't go."

- John Vizzuso

"I am me . . .no more. . .no less."

- John Vizzuso

"The price of success is measured in one's own self."

- John Vizzuso

"Surround yourself with good people and you'll win the battle. Surround yourself with great people and you'll win the war."

- John Vizzuso

"If you control your quality, then you will control your success."

- John Vizzuso

"If you wait an extra 25 minutes in the shower because you don't want to go to work, then it's time for a new job."

- John Vizzuso

"Performance appraisals are like paying taxes, if you cheat and lie, you'll get penalized in the end."

- John Vizzuso

"It takes months to find a new customer. . .seconds to lose one."

- Unknown

"If you take one string and cut it with scissors then the cut is easy. If you take thousands of strings and put them together then you make a rope. The strings are not easily cut because they are working together."

- John Vizzuso

"A service is great only when the customer says it's great."

- John Vizzuso

"Customer service is a lost magic."

- John Vizzuso

"A good manager will be able to promote somebody who can pick their nose and can fire their best friend."

- John Vizzuso

"Self trust is the first secret of success, so believe in and trust yourself."

- Unknown

"It's hard to be quoted when you are silent."

- John Vizzuso

"Do not follow the path where it may lead. Go instead where there is no path and leave a trail."

- Image Master

"All men die but not all men really live."

- William Wallace

"Open communication is a gift too often forgotten."

- John Vizzuso

"Immortality is a prize best left in the recesses of the mind."

- John Vizzuso

"If I ever give up again, I'll be living in a pine box six feet under."

- John Vizzuso

"Leadership is the key to succeed in management."

- John Vizzuso

"Live each day as if it was your last breath."

- John Vizzuso

"Educational degrees make graduates not good managers."

- John Vizzuso

"Don't fire them. . .fire them up."

- Frank Pacetta

"Every day remind yourself of your own abilities, of your good mind and affirm that you can make something really good out of your life."

- Unknown

"Work for a purpose, not money."

- John Vizzuso

"A company without customer service isn't really a business, but the thought in the head of a mad man."

- John Vizzuso

"Trying to separate management from customer service is like separating Siamese Twins that are attached at the head. . .you get brain failure and death."

- John Vizzuso

"Good judgment is the product of experience. Experience is the product of bad judgment."

- John Vizzuso

"Patience is a virtue in life, a must in hiring."

- John Vizzuso

"I've wooed, I've won and I'm done."

- John Vizzuso

"It's a mess-up like a soup sandwich."

- Carl Kozlowski

"Hire slow and fire fast."

- Al Van Kirk

"The ear of the leader must ring of the people."

- Woodrow Wilson

"You're measured by the difference you make."

- John Vizzuso

" A great leader's courage to fulfill the vision comes from the passion, not position."

- Unknown

"Adaptability is like flowing water, become your environment."

- John Vizzuso

At the Leadership Edge:
Beyond the Glory

"Immortality is a prize best left in the recesses of the mind."
J. Vizzuso

I can't believe that I am at the end of this book. It has taken over a year to write it, through some hard times. I wrote about all the things that can make a leader successful in business. I've discussed communication to relationships to defeating the beast on the battlefield. I saved this chapter for last because everything in life has a distinct price no matter what it is. A mother has to go through pain to give birth and produce a new life. The price of success in leadership is a steep one and one that I have paid dearly.

I told my wife about this chapter and she laughed out loud and said, "I should be writing that chapter." I need to finish the story from the first chapter. I got into my van and proceeded to do my job. If you remember, I just told my wife that I was leaving, which was going to end our relationship. I drove this van in the black of night with tears running down my cheeks. I could not believe I was allowing my life to fall apart, but I could not deal with the issues any longer.

The next day I rose from bed and went to work. I was having lunch at a local mall the next day when two young teenagers walked up to me.

They were representing a local Baptist church. They had a small booklet with them and they wanted to preach the word of God to me.

I agreed and they sat down and started going through this book. I began to get angry with each word they said. I had to stop them half way through the book. I looked at them and asked how old they were. The boy was 18 and the girl was 17. I asked them if they ever had anything tragic happen in their life. They claimed they had a grandfather die several years ago. I again asked them if anything really tragic happened in their lives. They claimed no to that question. I then handed them my business card and told them if something tragic ever happened to call me and tell me how much faith they have in their God then. I got up and left the table and went back to work.

Later that day a friend came up to me at work. She stated that she had a dream and did the word "Butch" have any meaning to me. This questioned really hit me hard. I told her that it was the nick name my father would call me. She stated she had a dream of a man saying this word but could not remember much about the dream other then there was a message she couldn't remember.

That night I had a very real dream. It was one of those dreams that seemed as real as my heart beating. My father was holding Laken. He looked at me and smiled and said, "Butch everything is going to be ok, she is with me." As I drove to work the next day, something hit me hard about my wife, son and my deceased daughter. I still had so many emotions stuck deep down inside which made it difficult for me to see clearly. The truth of the matter was that I was bent on being a strong leader, when in fact I left my wife horribly alone through this tragedy. The horrible truth now came to me in waves of frustration. My strength and ability not to give up were destroying my wife.

The guilt hit me – the thought of my wife alone these last few years, as I did nothing to stop it. I felt ashamed of who I was and where I was going. I could not believe that it was me all along – I gave up on Jennifer the night Laken died.

I decided that very moment, my wife needed me more now than ever and I would do whatever it took to make things better. I decided at that moment that I would not leave her again and I would release these emotions once and for all. I drove back that night and started the road to recovery – we've been happy ever since.

I learned a very valuable lesson from this experience. Leadership is not what you portray to others; it is what you portray to yourself. I wasn't leading my family, I was leading myself. It transformed me into a true leader, not one I thought I was. It made me realize that if you do not adapt to situations, the situations will adapt you.

I started to try and repair the life that I was so used to forgetting. I now had a different outlook on my business life. There had been so many times that I would lose myself in the business. I would be tempted by things of the world and try to hold my own. Success to me didn't constitute my becoming a business tycoon, but becoming the true man that I was, for without my family I was nothing. The money and success became a true void for me. In fact, I would give it all up if I could have my daughter back.

My business career carried on as I continued to fix my marriage and my life. I realized that I could have a balance and still succeed in business as well as my personal life. I felt an urge to make a difference in business and in my life, not to prove myself, but to help others understand what it means to succeed in business and life. I wanted to use my skills to help others become successful in their own rights. I wanted immortality in business and in my personal life.

What is the true price of success in business and in life? The true price of success is becoming the true person with one's inner-self and leaving all the inner demons behind. Believe in all that is good and forget all that is bad. It's being able to leave work in the recesses of business and living your life to its fullest. I cannot ever forgive myself for things I did in the past as far as the business is concerned, but part of the price is leaving those memories in the past and forging forward into the future.

Please don't get me wrong. All the things I wrote about being a leader are true and correct. You cannot have true success in anything, if first you don't realize who you are and what truly is important in your life.

You have to be able to look in the mirror and see and respect the person staring back at you.

I wrote a friend a short story one day that expressed what this friend has done for me. I learned a lot from this friend and will never forget this person for as long as I will live.

A man was walking down a long and narrow path. The path was mostly uphill and curved as no other. The man was wearing a weight pack on his back. He carried in it many things. He carried all his successes, resentments, failures, dreams and desires. The pack's straps were cutting into the flesh of his shoulders and made it painful for him to walk. He had no idea where he was going, but knew he had to keep moving or he would die a horrible death.

He had not eaten for days, for he had eaten his last meal many miles behind him. He walked up behind a large boulder and heard the cries of an animal. He turned the corner of the big rock and saw a bird caught in a hunter's snare. The bird was trapped in the snare and could not move. It was a beautiful bird, with bright colors and accents. The man was starving; he stood looking at the bird. His hands grabbed the bird and took it from the snare and he looked into its eyes. Its eyes were soft blue and looked deep within his eyes. There was pure love within those eyes, which made his soul feel warm.

In one swift move he released the bird to fly into the deep blue of the sky and it soared high and fast. In a bright flash of light, the man could see then that he was in a field with a large house in the middle. He walked up to the house and there stood a woman with her blonde hair flowing in the breeze of the day. Her eyes were a soft blue color. She wore a black Harley Davidson shirt, holding a book in her hand. She looked at him the same way the bird did. He stared at her, as though she was not there.

"What ya starin at ya freak!" she laughed as her one eyebrow raised "Hey goofy, dinner's on the table. Come in and wash up." He smiled and took his first step into the house and noticed something that hit him. The pack was gone, he walked without any pain. The difference he made for the bird released him from the pains of his inner soul. He walked into the rest of his life.

My life so far has been riddled with confusion and hardship, yet I have survived. I have combined the wisdom beyond my time to enhance my leadership style and success. It definitely was a process from the beginning until the present. I have realized that success is empty without purpose. It is meaningless without being happy in the personal life I call home.

Actually, through my experience and growth, I have realized that proving myself to my peers, to my family and to the beast is over. I strive everyday to make a difference not only in the lives of my employees, but in the lives of my family.

The difference I make will forever make me immortal within their eyes.

I can safely say that all my past experiences have molded me into the man I am today. When the sun shines in the morning and I look into the mirror, I see a man who has grown within himself and is proud at what he has become. I can then look up at the sky above, smile and say with a full heart,

"Thanks Pop!"

www.ingramcontent.com/pod-product-compliance
Lightning Source LLC
Chambersburg PA
CBHW032017170526
45157CB00002B/743